Indian Predictive

Fools obey planets, z

An ancient Indian proverb

Predictive Astrology is not an art of fortune-telling. Contrary to the popular belief, it is an organised and a systematic body of knowledge with its own time-tested principles and well-developed rules. In ancient India it was studied as a part of the *Vedas* (a *Vedanga*) and cultivated to a high degree of perfection. It represents an accumulation of knowledge and insights into correlations that exist between planetary movements, the cosmic rhythms, and the events and happenings that shape our lives.

Based on the influence of the Ascendant, the *Janma Nakshatras,* and other planetary combinations, Predictive Astrology identifies the inherent capabilities of an individual and provides the freedom to select a course of action best suited to one's strengths.

In simple language, the book explains how to choose favourable options in education, career, profession and business; to predict wealth and prosperity, success in love, romance and marriage, the state of health and longevity, and happiness and harmony in life. It provides guidelines to convert opportunities to advantage. It thus enables us to be a master, rather than be a prisoner of our destiny — and therein lies the critical importance of Indian Predictive Astrology and of this book.

The Author

The author, Dr V.K. Sharma, has spent more than 25 years studying and exploring astrological systems and their prognostications. His probings and significant contribution to astrology have been acknowledged in the form of several honorary titles being bestowed on him.

A regular contributor to magazines such as *The Astrological Magazine, Occult India, Jyotishmati* and *Jyotisha Tantra Rahasya,* Dr Sharma has delivered numerous lectures on astrology, occultism and mysticism. A telling example of the accuracy of his predictions was an article published in *Occult India* in August 1988, in which he foretold of danger to Rajiv Gandhi's life through 'fire and explosions'. *Sugama Phalita Jyotisha* is a widely read book on astrology written by him in Hindi.

By profession, a professor of Botany at the M.L. Sukhadia University at Udaipur, Dr Sharma also heads the Srividya Astro-Research Centre at Udaipur.

INDIAN PREDICTIVE ASTROLOGY

The Easy and Accurate Way to Interpret Your Future

Prof. Vishnu Sharma

Orient Paperbacks
DELHI | MUMBAI | HYDERABAD

There are many truths of which the full meaning cannot be realised until personal experience has brought it home.

—*John Stuart Mil*

ISBN : 978-81-222-0188-8

Indian Predictive Astrology: The Easy and Accurate Way to Interpret Your Future

Subject: Body, Mind & Spirit / Astrology

1st Published 1996
9th Printing 2013

Published by
Orient Paperbacks
(A division of Vision Books Pvt. Ltd.)
5A/8 Ansari Road, New Delhi-110 002
www.orientpaperbacks.com

Cover design by Vision Studio

Printed at
Anand Sons, Delhi-110 092, India

Cover Printed at
Ravindra Printing Press, Delhi-110 006, India

Contents

PART - I

The Indian System of Astrology

PART - II

Astrological Predictions

PART -III

Planetary Influences

Publisher's Note

Since this is a book on Indian Predictive Astrology, it is pertinent to point out that there are some definite differences between the Indian system of astrology and the Western system.

A major difference, among others, is that the date of entry of the Sun into each zodiac sign differs in the two systems. For example, according to the Indian system, the Sun enters Aries on or about April 14, whereas, in the Western system, the Sun enters Aries on March 21. The Indian system has been followed in this book.

Words in italics are Hindi/Sanskrit terms frequently used in astrology. Their English equivalents are given and explained both in the text and the glossary.

Part One

The Indian System of Astrology

1

Astrology: Study of the Preordained

Astrology is the most ancient of all knowledge. It demonstrates that celestial bodies exert a definite influence over all organic life on earth. Astrology reveals the characteristics of an individual, his positive and negative traits, successes and failures, position and status, education, chances of furthering his prospects, profits and losses, and so on. Thus, astrology helps an individual to understand himself, his family, and friends. It foretells the diseases, misfortunes, and dangers likely to be encountered. In a nutshell, astrology points out the potentialities, capabilities, and limitations of an individual. When properly understood, it is useful in day-to-day life. With the help of astrology, and by using a little intelligence, one can convert opportunity to one's advantage.

Astrology is practical astronomy and, in fact, one step ahead, as it seeks to trace the relationship between planets and stars, and their effects on human affairs. Astrology is not only a science — it is a philosophy as well, for it seeks to show that each and every human being has an appointed or preordained destiny to fulfil. It is from the study of the horoscope that an astrologer can accurately determine the character, opportunities, and destiny of the subject of the horoscope. None can choose for himself a destiny contrary to the one preordained for him.

Mark the words of Alexandre Dumas in this respect:

> There is in the life of every man an instant which decides his entire future. Although this moment is so important, it is rarely calculated or directed by the will. Almost always it is a chance which takes the man, like the wind does a leaf, and throws him into a new and unknown channel where, once he has entered it, he is obliged to obey a superior force, and where, quite believing he is following his own free will, he becomes the slave of circumstances and the plaything of events.

An individual's horoscope does contain the information that may enable an astrologer to forecast the exact period in which that opportunity is likely to present itself. And this is the wonderful and useful aspect of astrology.

Astrology is very different from occultism. In occultism, a study of the horoscope or a knowledge of the stars is not essential. All that is needed by an occultist is his psychic power on which he depends for his predictions. Astrology, on the other hand, makes a precise study of the position and interrelationship of the stars and planets on the basis of which an astrologer offers predictions.

The difference between Indian and Western astrology is that the Indian System tries to explain events, good or bad, based on past actions (*karmas*) of an individual, while the Western System focusses its attention mainly on character analysis and self-improvement of the native.

Branches of Predictive Astrology

Predictive astrology is based on the drawing up and reading of an individual's birth chart or horoscope. Ancient astrologers referred to this all-important part of astrology as *Jataka Shastra* or Native Astrology.

Predictions regarding a specific question are based on the time of the query and fall under *Prashna Shastra* or Horary Astrology.

Progressed horoscopy deals with casting and interpretation of an annual horoscope. It is known as *Varsha Phala*.

This book deals with the main branch of astrology — namely, Native Astrology.

The Solar System

The Sun is one of the stars of our galaxy and is the head of a family of nine planets — Mercury, Venus, Earth, Mars, Jupiter, Saturn, Uranus or Herschel, Neptune, and Pluto, arranged in order of their distance from the Sun. In reality, the Sun is stationary. It occupies a central position in the solar system and all planets including the Earth revolve around it. All planets rotate on their own axes and also revolve around the Sun in long elliptical orbits.

The Moon is one-fourth the size of the Earth, and is a satellite of the Earth. It revolves around the Earth in $27^1/_3$ days and also rotates on its own axis during the same time. Mercury is the smallest planet and is closest to the Sun. Venus is closest to the Earth and is slightly smaller than the Earth.

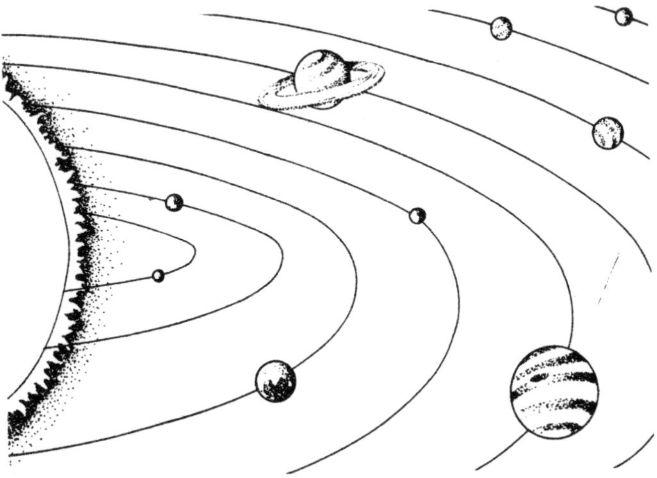

Fig. 1. The Solar System

Mars is slightly larger than Mercury. Jupiter is the largest planet in the solar system, Saturn is the second largest. Uranus, Neptune, and Pluto are larger than the Earth.

Revolution of Planets around the Sun

Planet	*Approx. Duration*
Mercury	88.00 days
Venus	224.70 "
Earth	365.26 "
Mars	687.00 "
Jupiter	11.86 years
Saturn	29.46 "
Uranus	84.01 "
Neptune	164.80 "
Pluto	247.70 "

Movement of the Earth: The Earth completes its circuit around the Sun in about 365 days. During this revolution, the solar orb is seen from the Earth through each one of the 12 zodiacal signs, one after the other. Thus the Earth moves from one sign of the zodiac to the other every month.

The Earth also rotates on its own axis from West to East every 24 hours. This causes all the 12 signs of the zodiac to pass over each portion of the Earth once in 24 hours. Therefore, in about every 2 hours, a new sign ascends over a given point of the Earth. Conversely, a given point on the Earth takes 2 hours to pass through a zodiacal sign.

The Zodiac: The path along which the Sun moves is called the ecliptic. In reality it is the pathway of the earth around the Sun. The broad belt extending to about 9° on either side of the ecliptic is known as the zodiac. The zodiac comprises 360° and for astrological purposes is divided into 12 equal parts called signs or *Rashis*. It is accepted that the zodiac commences from the first point of the sign Aries. The Zodiac revolves on its own axis, once in a day, from East to West. All the planets confine their lateral movements to the zodiac, which, for astrological purposes, is represented diagrammatically by a natal (birth) chart or horoscope.

Zodiac Signs: Each zodiacal sign (*Rashi*) is 30° in extent. Each degree of the sign is divided into 60 minutes and each minute is further sub-divided into 60 seconds. The signs are named after the constellations or stars. Since the zodiac is marked by 27 constellations and each constellation is of 13° -20', 2¼ constellations constitute a zodiacal sign. Each sign has its own peculiar qualities. It is among the signs of the zodiac that the planets wander.

English Name	*Hindi Name*	*English Name*	*Hindi Name*
Aries	*Mesha*	Libra	*Tula*
Taurus	*Vrishabbha*	Scorpio	*Vrishchika*
Gemini	*Mithuna*	Sagittarius	*Dhanu*
Cancer	*Karkataka*	Capricorn	*Makara*
Leo	*Simha*	Aquarius	*Kumbha*
Virgo	*Kanya*	Pisces	*Meena*

Planets: The term planet is derived from the Greek word planetes, meaning wanderers. A planet may be defined as a heavenly body travelling around the Sun in an approximately circular orbit. Unlike the stars which have fixed positions in the sky and are always visible, the planets change their positions and, sometimes, even disappear from view.

Celestial bodies considered as planets in astrology, though all of them are not planets in the true sense of the term are listed in the table on the following page, alongwith their symbols and names.

The Sun and Venus take about 30 days to move through a zodiacal sign. Mercury, being close to the Sun, is very unsteady in its movement. It completes its journey through a sign in about 27 days. The Moon takes about 54 hours; Mars, about 45 days; Jupiter, about 12 months; Saturn, about 30 months; and *Rahu* and *Ketu*, about 18 months to traverse through a sign. Unlike other planets which move in a clockwise direction (from West to East), *Rahu* and *Ketu* move in an anti-clockwise direction (from East to West).

Planets

English Name	*Hindi Name*	*Symbol*
The Sun*	*Ravi*	☉
The Moon*	*Chandra*	☾
Mars	*Mangala*	♂
Mercury	*Budha*	☿
Jupiter	*Guru*	♃
Venus	*Shukra*	♀
Saturn	*Shani*	♄
Uranus	*Indra.*	♅
Neptune	*Varuna*	♆
Dragon's Head*	*Rahu*	☊
Dragon's Tail*	*Ketu*	☋

It may be noted that Pluto has been left out from the above list of planets on account of its little-known effects on human affairs.

Retrogression and Acceleration: No two planets perform a complete revolution in the same period of time. Due to variations in their speed, one planet overtakes and passes another, thus giving the appearance of stopping and beginning to move backwards. This apparent stopping is referred to as 'stationary' and the apparent backward motion is called 'retrograde' *(Vakra).* No planet actually becomes stationary or retrograde. It is only an impression caused by the combined movement of planets and the Earth, and their positions in relation to the Sun. This can be compared to the trees which appear to be running when we see them from a moving train.

If a planet moves faster than its normal speed from one sign to the other, this phenomenon is called 'acceleration'. All planets, except the Sun and Moon, are subject to retrogression and acceleration in their orbits.

* Astronomically, the Sun and Moon are not planets but luminaries. They are, however, considered as planets in astrology. Similarly, *Rahu* and *Ketu* are not planets, though for purposes of prediction, they are considered as such. They are really the ascending and descending Nodes of the Moon, that is, the points at which the path of the Moon in the celestial sphere cuts that of the Sun.

Combustion: Planets in intimate conjunction with the Sun are subject to combustion *(Asta)* and become powerless. The Moon, Mars, Mercury, Jupiter, Venus, and Saturn become combust or eclipsed when they are respectively within 10^0, 11^0, 12^0, 14^0, 15^0, and 17^0 on either side of the Sun.

The Horoscope

The horoscope is a chart illustrating the positions of the Sun, Moon and other planets as well as the ascendant in various signs. It shows the exact position of the stars which each of the planets occupy at the time of birth.

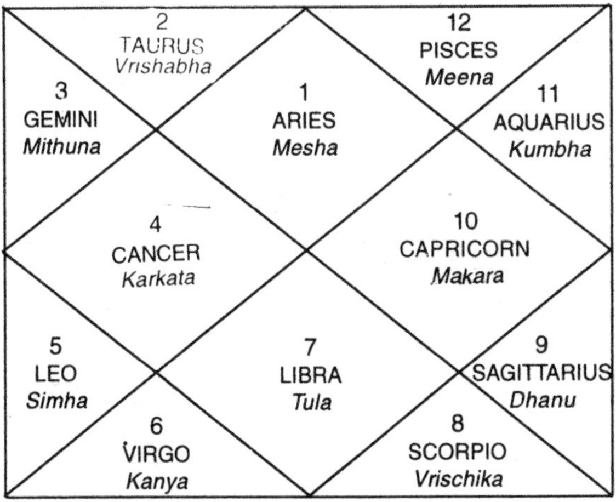

Fig. 2. The horoscope as drawn in Northern India

The sign that rises in the East at the time of birth is called the ascendant or *Lagna.* The ascendant in a horoscope is the epitome of a person's life.

In the Indian system of astrology, horoscopes are drawn in a square or an oblong form, whereas in the Western system, they are drawn in the form of a circle.

The difference between the North Indian and the South Indian horoscopes is, that in the former, the ascendant is always put at the top in the centre and the counting of the houses is done in the anticlockwise direction.

12 PISCES *Meena*	1 ARIES *Mesha*	2 TAURUS *Vrishabha*	3 GEMINI *Mithuna*
11 AQUARIUS *Kumbha*			4 CANCER *Karkata*
10 CAPRICORN *Makara*			5 LEO *Simha*
9 SAGITTARIUS *Dhanu*	8 SCORPIO *Vrischika*	7 LIBRA *Tula*	6 VIRGO *Kanya*

Fig. 3. The horoscope as drawn in other parts of India

In the South Indian horoscopes, on the other hand, the positions of several signs are fixed, but the position of the ascendant is changeable. The counting of houses is done in the clockwise direction, starting from the ascendant. In the South Indian charts the numbers denoting the signs are not written while in the North Indian charts the *Lagna* and other houses are indicated by putting the numbers of respective signs in places.

The Indian horoscopes are called *Nirayana* charts as opposed to the *Sayana* charts drawn in the Western countries as explained overleaf. A horoscope contains 12 houses and each house signifies certain important events and incidents. A horoscope cast as per the Western method can be converted into an Indian type by subtracting the *Ayanamsha* of the year of the birth from the longitudes of the cusps of the ascendant and houses.

Ayanamsha: *Ayanamsha* (precessional distance) is the distance between the first point of Aries and the Vernal Equinox.[1] The Indian astronomers consider the Vernal

1. The phenomenon of vernal equinox occurs every year on 21st March (as per the Gregorian Calender), when the Sun crosses the celestial equator, thus marking the first point of the sign Aries.

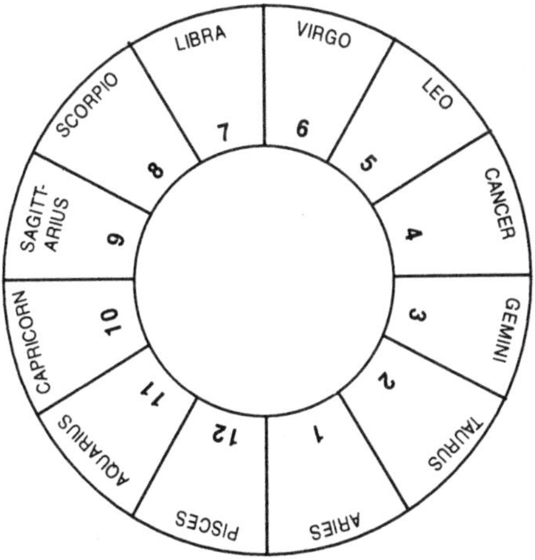

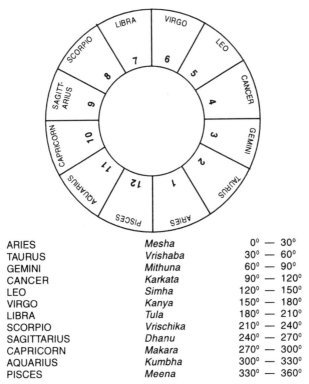

ARIES	*Mesha*	0° — 30°
TAURUS	*Vrishaba*	30° — 60°
GEMINI	*Mithuna*	60° — 90°
CANCER	*Karkata*	90° — 120°
LEO	*Simha*	120° — 150°
VIRGO	*Kanya*	150° — 180°
LIBRA	*Tula*	180° — 210°
SCORPIO	*Vrischika*	210° — 240°
SAGITTARIUS	*Dhanu*	240° — 270°
CAPRICORN	*Makara*	270° — 300°
AQUARIUS	*Kumbha*	300° — 330°
PISCES	*Meena*	330° — 360°

Fig. 4. The horoscope as drawn in the Western System

Equinox as fixed or stationary while the Western astronomers consider it as moving in the backward direction. The *Nirayana* longitude plus the *Ayanamsha* indicate the *Sayana* longitude of any place.

***Sayana* and *Nirayana* Systems:** The system of astronomy that recognises the movable zodiac is called the *Sayana* (with precession) system. This system is followed by Western astrologers. The *Nirayana* (ex-precession system) is employed by the Indian astrologers who consider the zodiac as fixed, and not movable.

Seasons: According to Hindu astronomy there are six seasons as detailed here.

Season	*Corresponding Lunar Months*
Vasanta (Spring)	*Chaitra* and *Vaishakha*
Greeshma (Summer)	*Jyeshtha* and *Ashadha*
Varsha (Rainy)	*Shravana* and *Bhadrapada*
Sharad (Autumn)	*Ashwina* and *Kartika*
Hemanta (Winter)	*Mrigashirsha* and *Pausha*
Shishira (Declining winter)	*Magha* and *Phalguna*

Ayanas: *Uttarayana* is the period of six months when the Sun moves from the zodiacal sign Capricorn to the sign Gemini.

Dakshinayana is the period of six months when the Sun moves from the sign Cancer to the sign Sagittarius.

Samvat: A period of twelve lunar months comprising two fortnights — the bright fortnight or *Shukla Paksha* and the dark fortnight or *Krishna Paksha*. The first day or *tithi* of each fortnight is referred to as 1, the second *tithi* as 2, and so on.

In North India, the *Samvat* begins from the first *tithi* of the *Shukla Paksha* of the first lunar month, that is, *Chaitra Shukla Paksha* 1. In South India the *Samvat* begins with the first *tithi* of the *Shukla Paksha* of *Kartika*, that is, *Kartika Shukla Paksha* 1.

Solar and Lunar Months: The solar month denotes the time taken by the Sun to traverse from one sign of the zodiac to another. The solar months are named after the zodiacal signs.

Solar Month	*Corresponding Zodiacal Signs*
Mesha	Aries
Vrishabha	Taurus
Mithuna	Gemini
Karkataka	Cancer
Simha	Leo
Kanya	Virgo
Tula	Libra
Vrishchika	Scorpio
Dhanu	Sagittarius
Makara	Capricorn
Kumbha	Aquarius
Meena	Pisces

The lunar month has 30 lunar days or *Tithis,* counted from the New Moon to the next New Moon. The New Moon is a simple conjunction of the Sun and Moon, that is, when the Moon is situated between the Earth and the Sun.

Lunar Month	*Corresponding English Calendar Months*
Chaitra	March - April
Vaishakha	April - May
Jyeshtha	May - June
Ashadha	June - July
Shravana	July - August
Bhadrapada	August - September
Ashwina	September - October
Kartika	October - November
Mrigashirsha	November - December
Pausha	December - January
Magha	January - February
Phalguna	February - March

Pakshas: Each lunar month consists of two *Pakshas* — *Shukla* and *Krishna. Shukla Paksha* consists of the bright fortnight — that is, when the Moon is waxing. It is the period from the day after the New Moon to the day of the full Moon. The dark fortnight of the lunar month is called *Krishna Paksha* — that is, when the Moon is waning. It is the period from the day after the full Moon to the day of the New Moon.

Tithis: Each lunar day is called a *Tithi.* The commencement, duration, and ending of each *Tithi* depends upon the distance, measured in degrees, between the relative positions of the Sun and Moon, as viewed from the Earth. Fourteen lunar days or *Tithis,* whether in the bright or the dark half, have the same number - 1, 2, 3, 4, 5, 6, 7, 8, 9, 10, 11, 12, 13, and 14. The 15th *Tithi* in the bright half is called *Poornima* (day of the Full Moon). The 15th *Tithi* in the dark half is called *Amavasya* (day of the New Moon). It is the 30th day from the commencement of the lunar month.

The Lunar Month

Tithi	*Bright half of the month*	*Tithi*	*Dark half of the month*
1	0 - 12^0	1	180 - 168^0
2	12 - 24^0	2	168 - 156^0
3	24 - 36^0	3	156 - 144^0
4	36 - 48^0	4	144 - 132^0
5	48 - 60^0	5	132 - 120^0
6	60 - 72^0	6	120 - 108^0
7	72 - 84^0	7	108 - 96^0
8	84 - 96^0	8	96 - 84^0
9	96 - 108^0	9	84 - 72^0
10	108 - 120^0	10	72 - 60^0
11	120 - 132^0	11	60 - 48^0
12	132 - 144^0	12	48 - 36^0
13	144 - 156^0	13	36 - 24^0
14	156 - 168^0	14	24 - 12^0
15	168 - 180^0	15/30	12 - 0^0

2

Sun Signs

The ascendant or *Lagna* in a birth chart indicates the physical appearance of the individual. The Sun represents the soul, energy, and will-power. The Moon represents the mind and emotions. Unlike the ascendant, which is always the first house but may occupy any sign, the Sun and Moon can occupy any sign in any house of a horoscope. These three — the ascendant, the Sun, and the Moon — comprise the tripod on which the edifice of a person's destiny is built.

The earth revolves around the Sun, completing the circuit in one year. Though the Sun is stationary, each of the 12 signs of the zodiac comes under the direct influence of the Sun through the movement of the earth around the Sun. In astrological parlance, however, it is said that the Sun remains in a sign for about a month and the Moon for about 54 hours before moving on to the other signs. The astrological reading of a person's character and individuality may be judged by the Sun's position in relation to a sign at any given moment. In Indian astrology the position of the Moon in a sign at the time of birth is given great importance. On the other hand, in Western astrology, great emphasis is placed on the position of the Sun in a sign at the time of birth.

The general characteristics of persons born in different signs in which the ascendant and Moon may be deposited have been described later in the book. In the following paragraphs, the basic characteristics of persons according to the Sun's position in different signs have been delineated. Those persons who do not have a horoscope or do not know their Moon sign but only know their date of birth, can easily find out their basic characteristics by reading the following details. As mentioned earlier, the Sun stays in a sign for about a month. This period of the Sun's stay in a sign is called one Solar month. In the Indian and Western systems there is a great variation in the dates of the Sun's entry into each sign. For example, according to the Indian or *Nirayana* system, the Sun enters into Aries on or about April 14. But according to the Western or *Sayana* system, the Sun enters Aries on March 21. The Indian system has been followed in this book. The Sun's transit dates, as given below, are approximate. One can, however, find out the correct date of the Sun's entry into a particular sign by referring to the almanac of the desired year.

Aries (*Mesha*): Apr. 14-May 13 approximately: People born during this period of the year have a strong will-power, ambition, and courage. They do not like criticism, and lack tact and diplomacy. They are straightforward and do not care much for the feelings and sentiments of others. By nature they are impulsive and rash. They usually succeed in life, achieve a good position, and earn money. They are best suited for a career connected with metals, metallurgy, engineering, surgery, explosives, sports, and so on. Their love affairs are quick and sudden. However they are usually unhappy in their married life because they seldom understand their partners. Persons born during this period would do well to marry someone born between August 14 and September 13, or

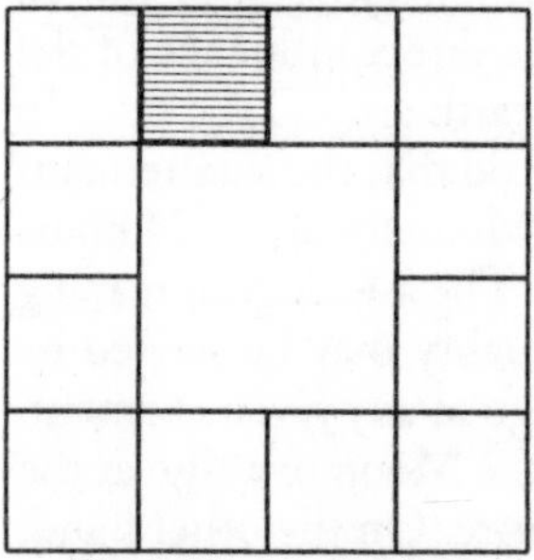

Fig. 5. The shaded box represents the Sun in Aries.

December 14 and January 13 of any year. The diseases from which Arians are likely to suffer from are headaches, eye troubles, and cuts and wounds in the head.

Taurus (*Vrishabha*): May 14-June 13 approximately: People born during this period of the year are dominating and obstinate. They are practical, successful, and trustworthy. They are generally patient and persevering, and have great powers of endurance. Taureans make faithful and loyal friends. They are very careful about their personal comforts and money matters. The jobs best suited to them are advertising, public relations, music, catering, banking, engineering, agriculture, to name a few. A native whose Sun is in the sign Taurus is a sensuous person, and very jealous and sentimental in matters of sex. He can be easily misled by emotions and affections. He is well advised to marry a person born between September 14 and October 13, or January 14 and February 13. He is inclined to suffer from diseases of the throat, nasal cavities, and upper part of the lungs.

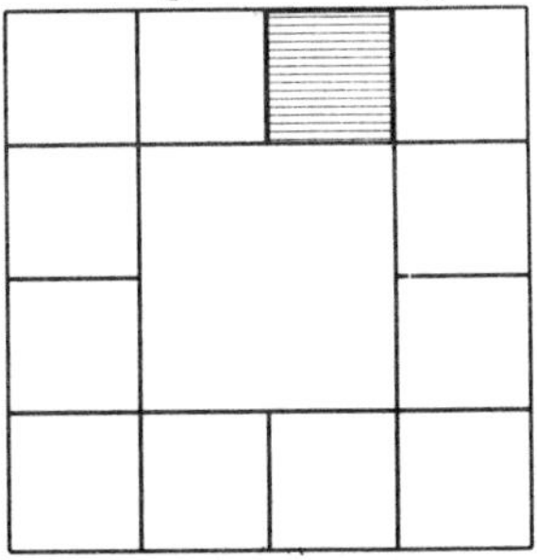

Fig. 6. The shaded box represents the Sun in Taurus.

Gemini (*Mithuna*): June 14-July 13 approximately: Persons born during this period possess a dual character and temperament. Their moods are easily changeable; and as a rule, they are restless, diplomatic, and ambitious. Being intellectual and versatile, they are suitable for a variety of careers, including teaching, journalism, publishing, selling, and acting. People with the Sun in Gemini are inconsistent in their love life. By nature they are flirtatious and have more than one affair. A Geminian is well advised to

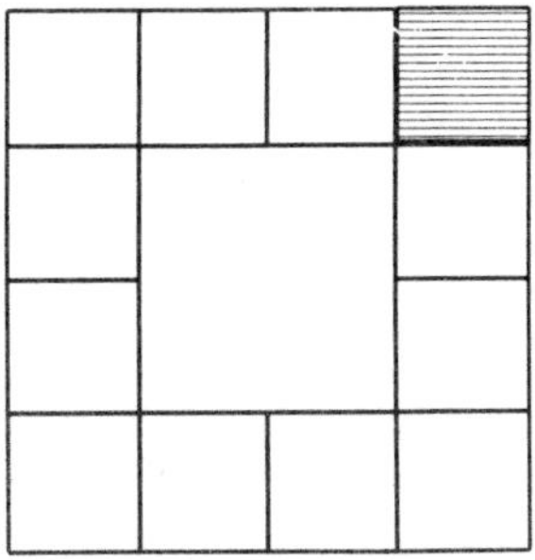

Fig. 7. The shaded box represents the Sun in Gemini.

marry a person born between October 14 and November 13, or between February 14 and March 13. Geminians are inclined to suffer from diseases of the nervous system, digestive organs, and chest.

Cancer (*Karkataka*): July 14-Aug. 13 approximately: People born during this period are changeable, sensitive, moody, and restless. They are emotional, tenacious in their feelings, and attached to their home and family. However, they seldom find domestic happiness. Being hard-working and industrious, they are usually successful in business. They often reach high positions in life. Success comes their way in a career connected with teaching, acting, banking, and selling. By nature they are romantic and of a very loving and affectionate disposition. Cancerians would do well to marry a person born between November 14 and December 13, or March 14 and April 13. These people are likely to suffer from gastric troubles, nervous depression, and inflammatory troubles.

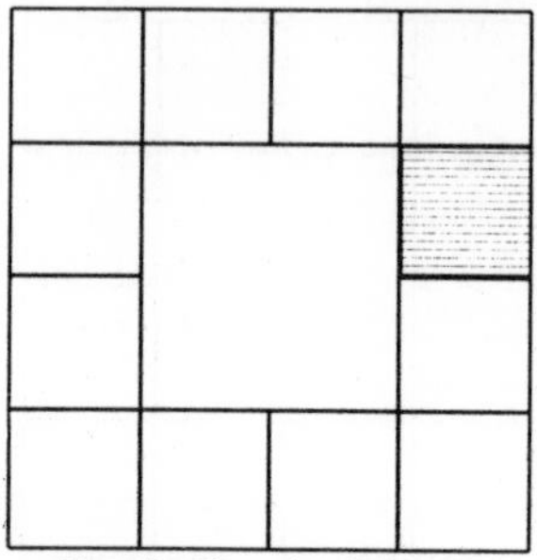

Fig. 8. The shaded box represents the Sun in Cancer.

Leo (*Simha*): Aug. 14-Sept. 13 approximately: Leos are extremely sympathetic, generous, honest, straightforward and authoritative. They are proud and lucky in money matters. They possess a strong will-power and great tenacity of purpose. They usually achieve their objective in spite of difficulties or obstacles. The careers best suited to them are the armed forces, civil services, finance, business, and politics. In matters of love they are possessive, passionate, and loyal. They crave for love which often eludes them

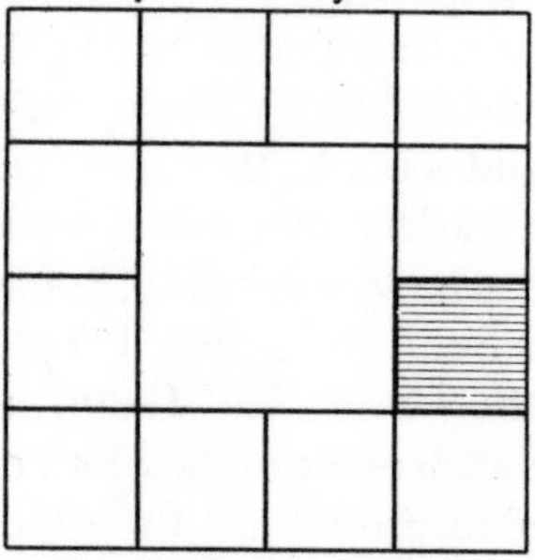

Fig. 9. The shaded box represents the Sun in Leo.

due to their stubborn temperament. Leos will find compatibility with a person born between December 14 and January 13, or April 14 and May 13. Leos are inclined to suffer from heart problems, and pain in the head and ears.

Virgo (*Kanya*): Sept. 14-Oct. 13 approximately: The Sun remains in the sign Virgo approximately between September 14 and October 13. People born during this period are generally successful in life. They possess good judgement and a keen analytical power. They are neither easily impressed nor deceived by others. They always try to maintain a high standard of living. Virgos can be successful in business, and are also capable of adapting themselves to numerous vocations such as banking, medicine, journalism, law, and telecommunications. On the emotional front, however, they are difficult to understand. Both strong and weak characters are found in this Sun sign. They should marry a person born between January 14 and February 13, or May 14 and June 13. Though Virgos are generally healthy, an inharmonious environment can affect them adversely. The diseases which they are likely to suffer from are chest troubles and neuritis of the shoulder and arm.

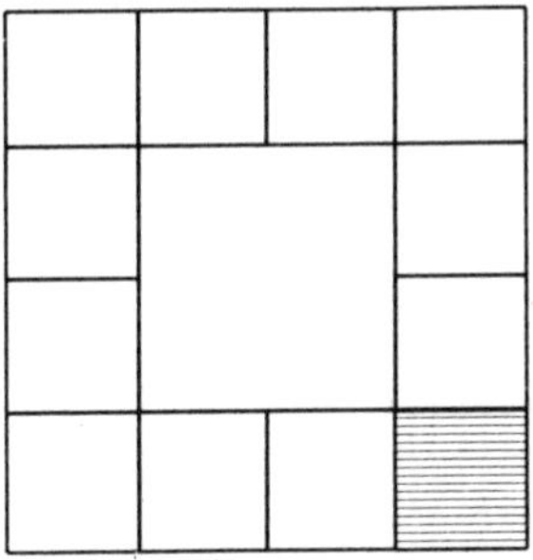

Fig. 10. The shaded box represents the Sun in Virgo.

Libra (*Tula*): Oct. 14-Nov. 13 approximately: The Sun remains in the sign Libra approximately between October 14 and November 13. Persons born during this period are decisive in their thoughts and actions. They have great foresight and intuition. They are diplomatic, alert, balanced, and just. They have a large circle of

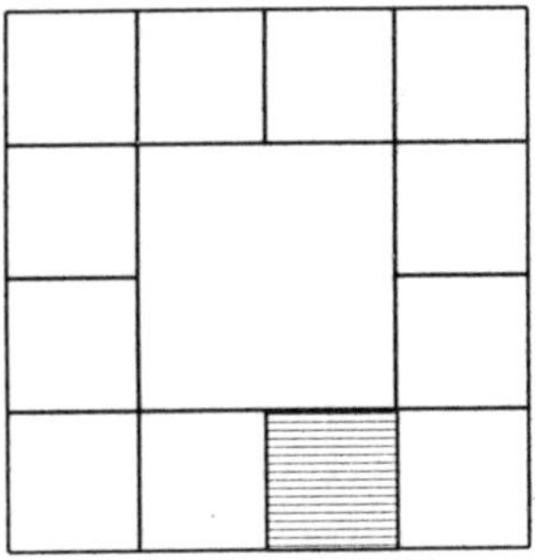

Fig. 11. The shaded box represents the Sun in Libra.

friends and acquaintances. All sorts of careers are suitable to them, though they are more successful as lawyers, judges, politicians, diplomats, and salespersons. They often hold a prominent position in public life. On the marital front, however, they are seldom happy. They would do well to marry a person born between February 14 and March 13, or June 14 and July 13. Those born during the solar month of *Tula* are inclined to suffer from pain in the back, kidneys, and head.

Scorpio (*Vrishchika*): Nov. 14-Dec. 13 approximately: The Sun usually remains in the sign Scorpio between November 14 and December 13. Persons born during this period are determined, independent, and energetic. They have a magnetic personality and are versatile. Paradoxically, the basest and noblest of persons are found in this sign. Scorpios usually lead a double life, one for themselves and another for others. They have clear ideas about business and politics. Scorpios make successful physicians, surgeons, detectives, researchers, psychiatrists, and military officers. They are very demanding in their sex life, and are dogmatic and dominating at home. They have as many friends as enemies. They should, preferably, marry a person born between March 14 and April 13, or July 14 and August 13. People born with the Sun in Scorpio are, as a rule, thin in their early years, but put on weight during middle age. They are inclined to suffer from diseases of the heart, lungs, and sex organs.

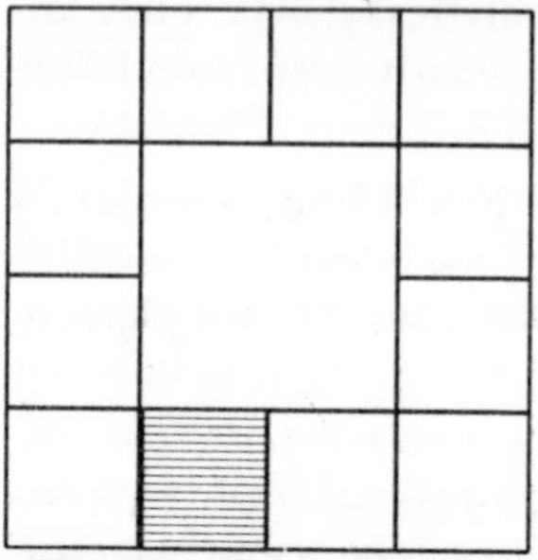

Fig. 12. The shaded box represents the Sun in Scorpio.

Sagittarius (*Dhanu*): Dec. 14-Jan. 13 approximately: People born during this period are enthusiastic, determined, and impulsive. They are usually outspoken and, thus, make many enemies. Being honest themselves, Sagittarians resent deception. They are friendly and sociable. They usually go to the extremes in all things and make sudden decisions.

However, they are successful at whatever they do. They are best suited to a career connected with teaching, writing, publishing, research, defence, and sports. They usually marry on impulse and are seldom happy in their married life. They are advised to marry a person born between April 14 and May 13, or August 14 and September 13. These people are inclined to suffer from rheumatism and diseases of the nervous system.

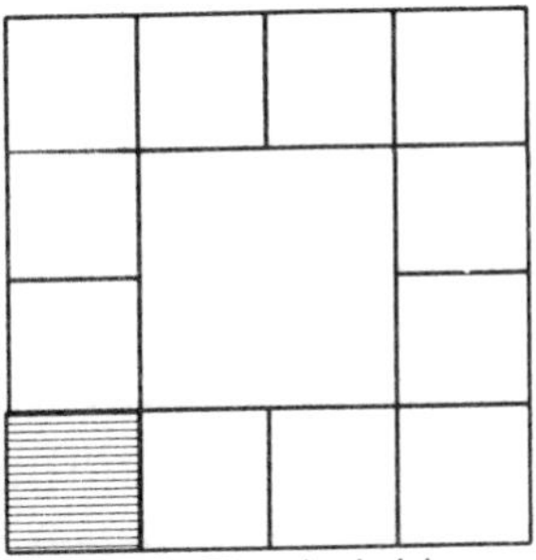

Fig. 13. The shaded box represents the Sun in Sagittarius.

Capricorn (*Makara*): Jan. 14-Feb. 13 approximately: The Sun usually remains in Capricorn between January 14 and February 13. People born during this period are mentally strong, determined, and independent in all their actions. Apart from being hard-working, they are thinkers too. They can excel in any work that requires administrative or managerial skills, including government service, commerce, agriculture, engineering, and education. They neither interfere with the affairs of others, nor tolerate interference by others. Their temperament is somewhat melancholic and, therefore, generally misunderstood by others. Family life for Capricornians is, usually, a troubled one. They are advised to marry a person born between May 14 and June 13, or September 14 and October 13. They are likely to suffer from liver troubles, rheumatism, and pain in the feet.

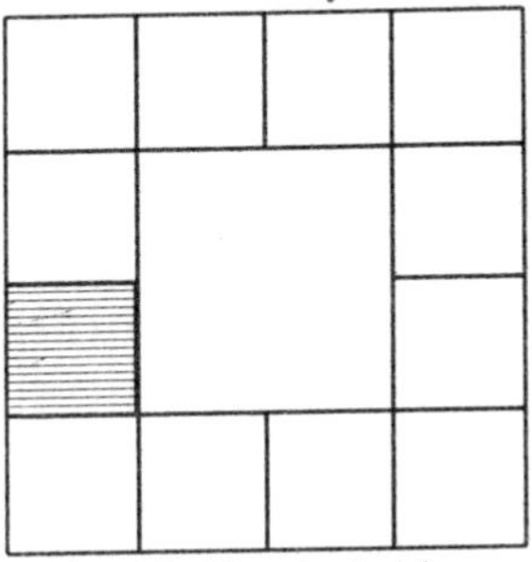

Fig. 14. The shaded box represents the Sun in Capricorn.

Aquarius (*Kumbha*): Feb. 14-Mar. 13 approximately: Aquarians are over-sensitive and their feelings are easily hurt. They often lose control of themselves and say or do things

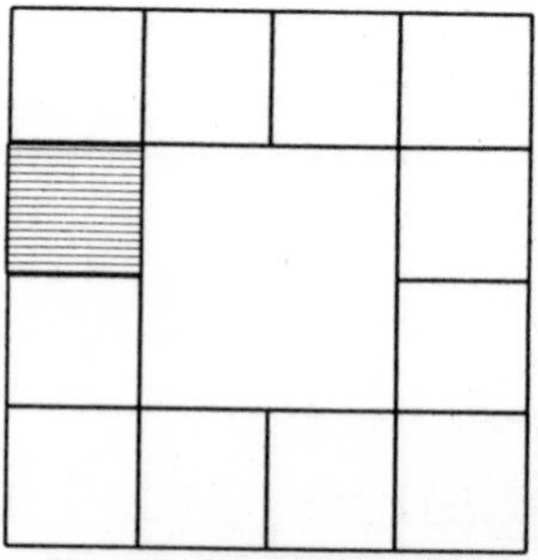

Fig. 15. The shaded box represents the Sun in Aquarius.

which they regret later. Though they are sociable, they suffer from loneliness in life. They do, however, make good friends and wise counsellors. Persons with Aquarius as their Sun sign are successful at debates and arguments. They have a scientific bent of mind, and are successful as doctors, writers, actors, scientists, and psychologists. They take great interest in public meetings and ceremonies. In their personal life, they often indulge in clandestine love affairs and are, therefore, unhappy in their married life. They would do well to marry a person born between June 14 and July 13, or October 14 and November 13. They are inclined to suffer from gastric and circulatory diseases.

Pisces (*Meena*): Mar. 14-Apr. 13 approximately: Those born during this period are generous, sympathetic, and kind. They have a tendency to brood and become melancholic. They are loyal to their friends or to any cause they take up, provided they feel they are trusted. They are generally successful in all positions of responsibility, but are best suited for a career connected with education, journalism, astrology, occultism, poetry, and acting. Pisceans have a strong desire to love and be loved. Quite often, this leads them to carry on with a romance secretly. They are advised to marry a person born between July 14 and August 13, or November 14 and December 13. People born during the month of *Meena* have a dual personality. The strongest and weakest characters are found in this sign. They are mostly inclined to suffer from nervous depression, insomnia, anaemia, and eye trouble.

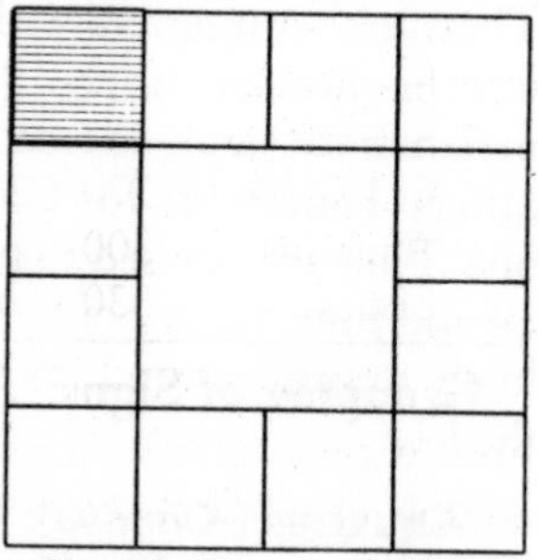

Fig. 16. The shaded box represents the Sun in Pisces.

3

Houses of the Zodiac: Their Significance

As explained in Chapter 1, there are twelve parts of the zodiac, called signs or *Rashis*. Each sign of the zodiac is 30° in extent. The zodiacal signs are tabulated as below:

Zodiac Signs

Sign	*Extent*	*Represented by*	*No. Denoting the Sign*
Aries	0 - 30°	Ram	1
Taurus	30 - 60°	Bull	2
Gemini	60 - 90°	Pair of lovers	3
Cancer	90 - 120°	Crab	4
Leo	120 - 150°	Lion	5
Virgo	150 - 180°	Maiden	6
Libra	180 - 210°	Balance	7
Scorpio	210 - 240°	Scorpion	8
Sagittarius	240 - 270°	Bow	9
Capricorn	270 - 300°	Crocodile	10
Aquarius	300 - 330°	Pot	11
Pisces	330 - 360°	Pair of fish	12

Grouping of Signs: The signs can be categorised into three groups from Aries onwards. They are termed as movable or cardinal, fixed, and common or mutable. Movable signs indicate an energetic and dynamic nature; fixed signs, a tenacious and stubborn nature; and common signs, a changeable nature.

Movable	*Fixed*	*Common*
Aries	Taurus	Gemini
Cancer	Leo	Virgo
Libra	Scorpio	Sagittarius
Capricorn	Aquarius	Pisces

Each sign starting from Aries onwards is also sequentially termed as odd (or male) and even (or female). All odd signs are cruel and masculine and all even signs are mild and feminine.

Odd	*Even*
Aries	Taurus
Gemini	Cancer
Leo	Virgo
Libra	Scorpio
Sagittarius	Capricorn
Aquarius	Pisces

The signs can also be divided into four groups, representing the basic elements — fire, earth, air, and water. Thus the signs starting from Aries onwards are termed sequentially as fiery, earthy, airy, and watery.

Fiery	*Earthy*	*Airy*	*Watery*
Aries	Taurus	Gemini	Cancer
Leo	Virgo	Libra	Scorpio
Sagittarius	Capricorn	Aquarius	Pisces

Houses

The twelve divisions of the zodiac are also called houses or *Bhavas*. The position of the zodiac signs at the time of birth vary from one individual to another. For example, if a person is born with Leo as the rising sign, it becomes the first house (as different from the signs of the zodiac — when it is the fifth sign, when Aries is taken as the first sign). Any one of the twelve signs rising on the Eastern horizon at the time of the birth of an individual is called the rising sign or ascendant *(Lagna)*. The sign next to the rising sign or *Lagna* is the 2nd house, the 3rd sign from the rising sign is the 3rd house, and so on. Thus, in every horoscope there are 12 houses and each house is 30° in extent. Each of the 12 houses will have a different value and significance for each individual, according to his date and time of birth. In the Western system, however, all houses are not of 30°. They vary according to the latitude[1] of the place and time of birth.

The longitude[2] of a house is the beginning point of that house, that is, the 1st house begins from the longitude of the ascendant and extends up to the longitude of the 2nd house, from which point again, the 2nd house begins, and so on. Thus, the longitudes of the different houses are the junction points of the houses and, as such, they are called the cusps or *Sandhis* of the houses.

In the Indian method, the cusps or the longitudes of the houses are the middle points of the respective houses. A house begins from about 15° behind the longitude of that house and extends up to about 15° ahead of it. The longitudes of the houses are thus the middle points or *Sandhis* of those houses and are the most sensitive points in the horoscope. A house extends from the preceding *Sandhi* up to the following *Sandhi* of the concerned house.

Significance of the Houses: The twelve houses (as usually understood) in the horoscope signify different aspects of a man's life as given below:

House	*Significance*
First	Personality, body, face, appearance, health
Second	Wealth, speech, family, neck, throat, right eye
Third	Brother or sister, courage, short journeys, hands, right ear
Fourth	Education, mother, house or land, conveyance, general happiness, maternal uncle, chest
Fifth	Children, intelligence, fame, position, love, stomach

1. The distance measured north or south of the Ecliptic.
2. The distance measured along the Ecliptic.

Sixth	Diseases, debts, sorrows, injuries, notoriety, aunt or uncle, waist, enemies
Seventh	Marriage, desires, sexual diseases, loins
Eighth	Death or Longevity, sexual organs, obstacles, unearned wealth, accident
Ninth	Fortune, character, religion, father, long journeys, grandson, thighs
Tenth	Profession, father, rank, authority, honour, success, knees
Eleventh	Gains, fulfilment of desires, prosperity, friends, left ear, ankles
Twelfth	Losses, misery, expenditure, comforts of bed, salvation or *Moksha*, feet, left eye

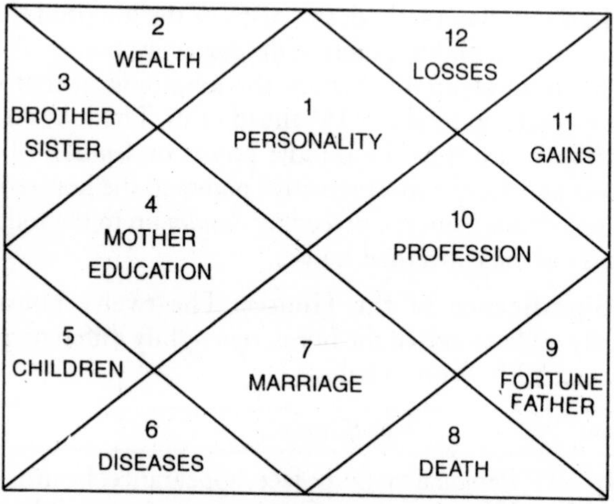

Fig. 17. Significance of the houses. The numbers 1-12 refer to the First house, Second house, and so on.

Grouping of Houses: The houses are variously grouped as follows:

- Quadrants or angles or *Kendras*: 1st, 4th, 7th and 10th houses.
- The 1st house, besides being a *Kendra*, is also a *Trikona.*

- Trines or *Trikonas*: 1st, 5th, and 9th houses.
- Succeedent or *Panapharas*: 2nd, 5th, 8th, and 11th houses.
- The 5th house is both a *Trikona* and a *Panaphara*.
- Cadent or *Apoklimas*: 3rd, 6th, 9th, and 12th houses.

The 9th house is both a *Trikona* and an *Apoklima*.

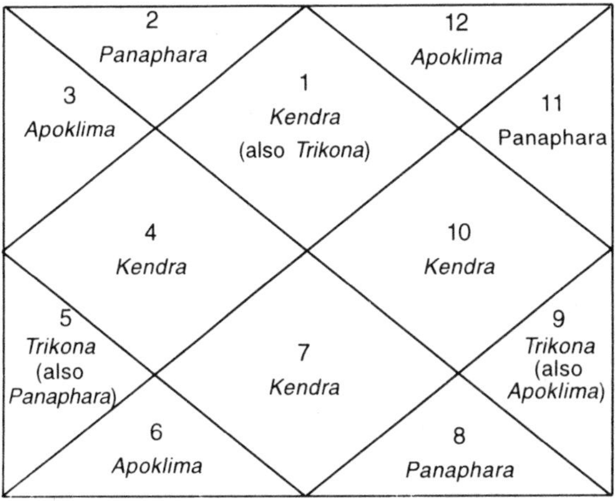

Fig. 18 Grouping of the houses. The numbers 1-12 refer to the First house, Second house, and so on.

In terms of a person's life, the *Kendras* denote childhood, the *Panapharas* denote middle age, and the *Apoklimas* denote old age. The 1st to 8th houses relate to one's material life, the 9th to 11th pertain to religious or moral beliefs, and the 12th house deals with the other world, that is, *Moksha*.

Favourable houses or *Upachayas*: 3rd, 6th, 10th, and 11th.

Death-inflicting houses or *Marakas*: 2nd and 7th.

Evil houses or *Trikas*: 6th, 8th and 12th.

Strength of a House: To determine the strength of a house[1], one must consider (1) the strength of the lord of that house; and (2) the strength of the dispositor, that is, the

1. Each house in permanently presided over by a planet which is said to govern the house or rule over it.

strength of the lord of the house in which the lord of the above is situated. The meaning of the word dispositor can best be explained with an example. Suppose in a Leo nativity, Mercury, as lord of the 2nd house, is in the 5th house and Jupiter is in the 6th house. Jupiter, as lord of the 5th house, would thus act as the dispositor of Mercury. The dispositor in this case is weak as Jupiter is occupying its debilitation sign. If the lord of the house and its dispositor are both powerful, the results of that particular house will be good. If one of them is powerful, the results of that particular house will be of mixed nature. If both of them happen to be weak and powerless, the results of that particular house will be bad.

The lords of trines are considered as first-rate benefics.

The lords of quadrants are considered as second-rate benefics.

The lords of the 2nd, 3rd, and 11th houses are considered as third-rate benefics or third-rate malefics. In other words, if the lords of the above-mentioned houses are associated with good planets, they are considered benefics; if associated with evil planets, they are considered malefics.

The lords of the 6th, 8th, and 12th houses are considered malefics.

A house may be considered as powerful if:

- The lord of that house is in a quadrant from that house, or from the ascendant, or from the lord of the ascendant.
- The lord of that house is in a trine from that house, or from the ascendant, or from the lord of the ascendant.
- The lord of that house is in the 3rd, 6th, 10th, or 11th house counted from the ascendant.
- The lord of that house is associated with or surrounded on both sides by benefic planets.
- The lord of that house is aspected by benefic planets.
- The lord of the sign occupied by the lord of that house is in its own, exaltation, or *Moolatrikona* sign.

A house may be considered as powerless if:

- Its lord occupies the 6th, 8th, or 12th house from the

ascendant, or from the lord of the ascendant, or from the house itself.

- Its lord is associated with or is in between malefic planets.
- Its lord is aspected by a malefic planet.
- Its lord is in an inimical sign.
- Its lord is in its debilitated sign.
- Its lord is under combustion by the Sun.
- The lord of the sign occupied by the lord of the house under consideration is in debilitation or an inimical state.

4

The Influence of Ascendants

When a child is born at any place, any one of the 12 signs of the zodiac will be rising at that time on the Eastern horizon. This rising sign is called the ascendant or *Lagna*. The ascendant may fall in any sign such as Aries, Taurus, Gemini, and so on. The personality or physical appearance and nature of the child will depend largely upon this rising sign.

The general characteristics of males born in different zodiacal signs as ascendant are described below. Characteristics pertaining to females are delineated in Chapter 15. Though these characteristics are too general and brief, yet they can certainly help in revealing the general aspects of one's personality. However, it must be remembered that a planet situated in the ascendant or aspecting it greatly, modifies the influence of the rising sign.

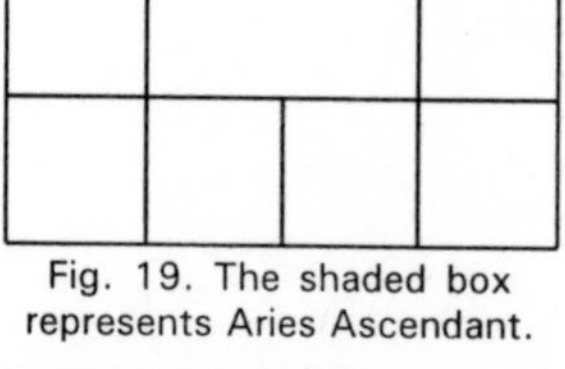

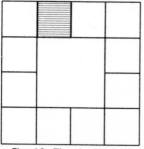

Fig. 19. The shaded box represents Aries Ascendant.

Aries: When the ascending sign or *Lagna* is Aries, the native has a middle-sized, strong

1. The ascendant (Asc.) refers to the sign that is rising in the East at the birth of a child.

muscular body and round eyes. He is active and independent. He is bold, capable, stubborn, frank, and ambitious. He is also sensitive, talkative, respectable, and fond of beauty and art. His wife is inclined to be lazy and proud, and he will have few children.

Taurus: A person born with Taurus as the ascendant is, usually, a short, thick-set person. He is essentially a lover of ease and comforts. He has a big face, broad forehead, and strong body. He is liberal and passionate, and possesses a cooperative nature. He will have few children. The Taurus-born is intelligent, learned, and has good writing skills. His wife will, probably, be beautiful and virtuous.

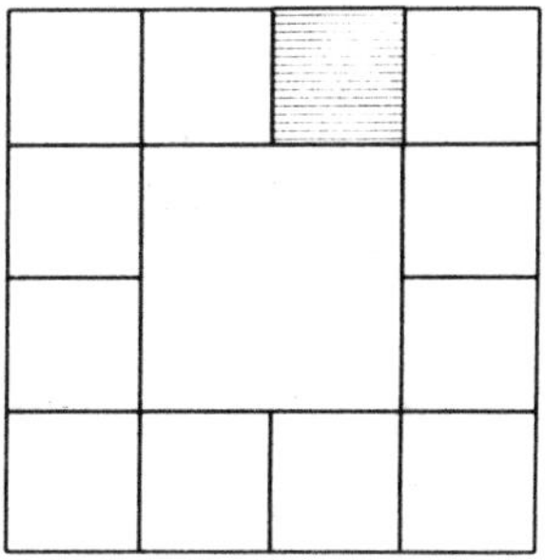

Fig. 20. The shaded box represents Taurus Ascendant.

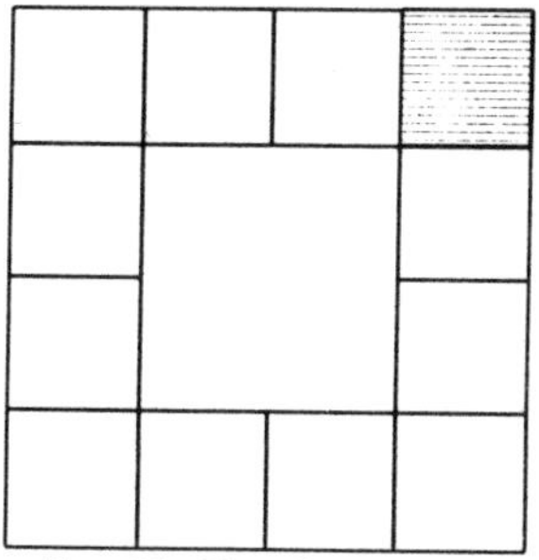

Fig. 21. The shaded box represents Gemini Ascendant.

Gemini: A person born with Gemini as the *Lagna* has a slender beautiful body, curly hair, and prominent nose. He is clever, fickle, and fond of sensual pleasure. He is a good conversationalist. However, he does not usually maintain good relations with his own relatives. His wife may be ill-tempered and unkind.

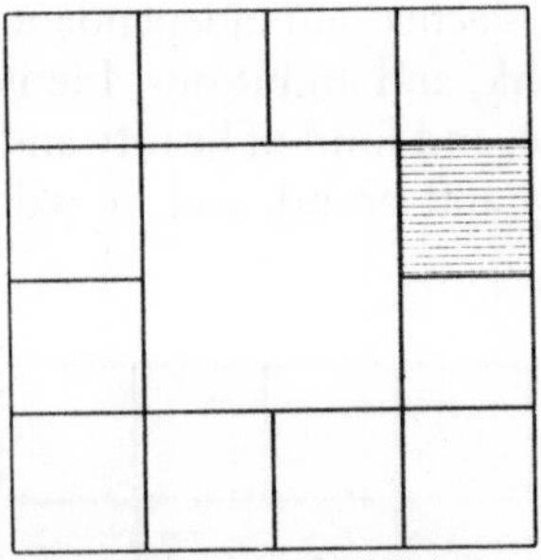

Fig. 22. The shaded box represents Cancer Ascendant.

Cancer: The Cancer-born has a middle-sized plump body. He is intelligent, industrious, and proud. He is honest, talkative, independent, and sensitive, but also miserly. He has a number of good friends but few children. His wife will be well-mannered and devoted.

Leo: The Leo-born is tall, bold, generous, and respectable. He has broad shoulders and is inclined towards quick anger. Success comes to him only after much struggle. He will remain devoted to his parents. His wife will be virtuous.

Fig. 23. The shaded box represents Leo Ascendant.

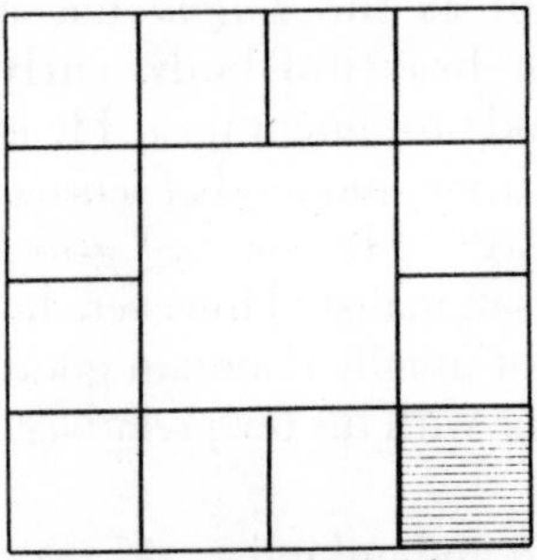

Fig. 24. The shaded box represents Virgo Ascendant.

Virgo: A person born with Virgo as the rising sign has a sharp intellect and a slender, middle-sized stature. He is impulsive, religious, and influential. He is fond of learning and may be interested in art, literature, or science. He is usually shy. His wife will be good-looking and devoted to him.

Libra: The Libra-born is lean and of middle height. He is clever at making schemes as he possesses a sound judgement. He is popular, and is a lover of art and female society. By nature he is practical. His wife will be of a quarrelsome nature.

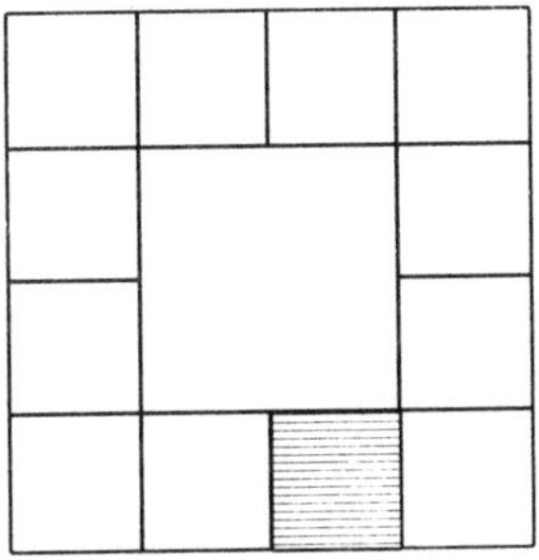

Fig. 25. The shaded box represents Libra Ascendant.

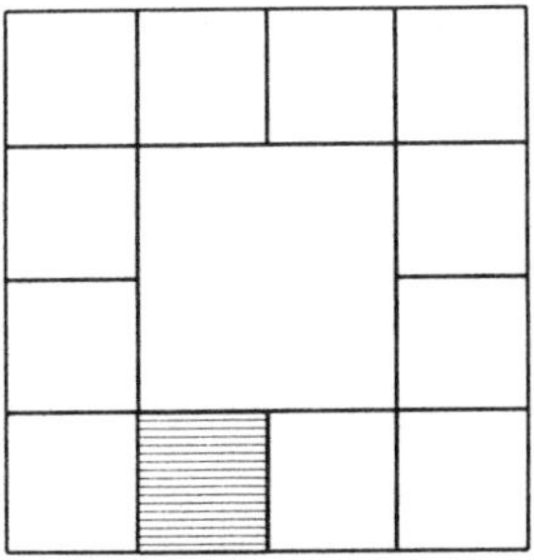

Fig. 26. The shaded box represents Scorpio Asc.

Scorpio: A person born with Scorpio as the ascendant has a well-set body and a middle stature. He has a youthful appearance and a fickle mind. He is clever, powerful, and dignified. He is cruel, sensual, and usually not generous. He is a good conversationalist and possesses equally good writing skills. His wife will be polite and obedient.

Sagittarius: The Sagittarius-born has a tall, corpulent body and attractive face. He is alert and intuitive. He has creative ability and is reliable. He has a high sense of honesty and justice. His wife will be bad tempered.

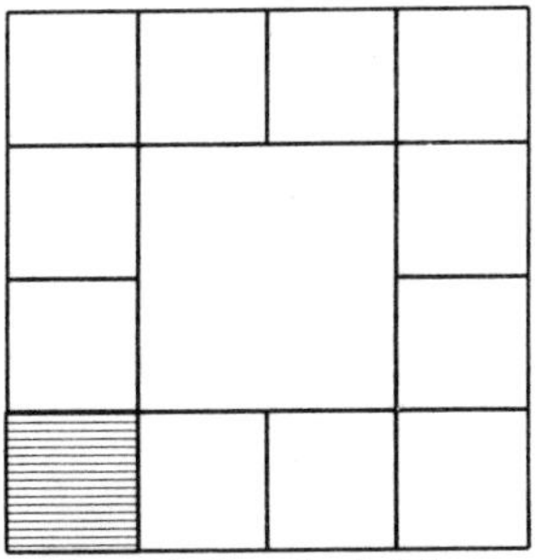

Fig. 27. The shaded box represents Sagittarius Asc.

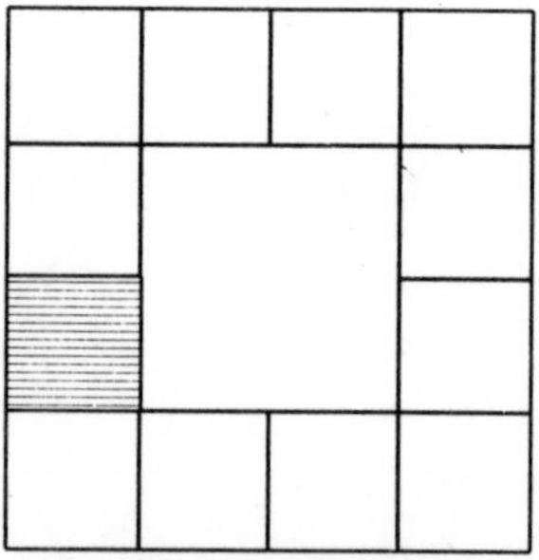

Fig. 28. The shaded box represents Capricorn Asc.

Capricorn: When the rising sign is Capricorn, the person is of middle-stature, clever, and fickle. He is able to adapt himself according to circumstances. He is strong-minded and very patient. He will have few children. His wife will be beautiful and happy-go-lucky.

Aquarius: The Aquarius-born is a middle-statured, strong person. He is talkative, happy, and stubborn. He is kind and fond of learning. His wife will be ill-tempered.

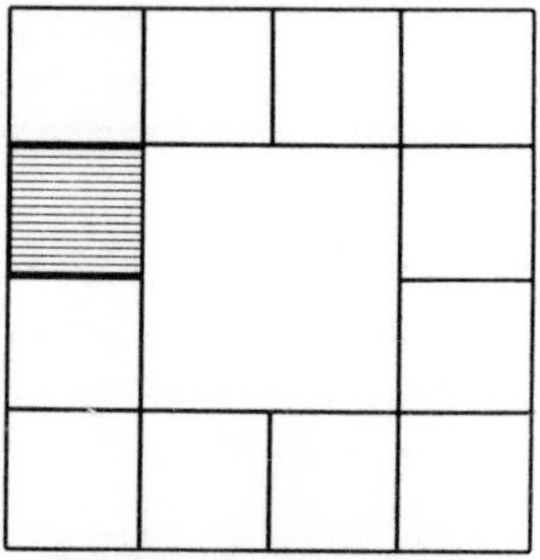

Fig. 29. The shaded box represents Aquarius Asc.

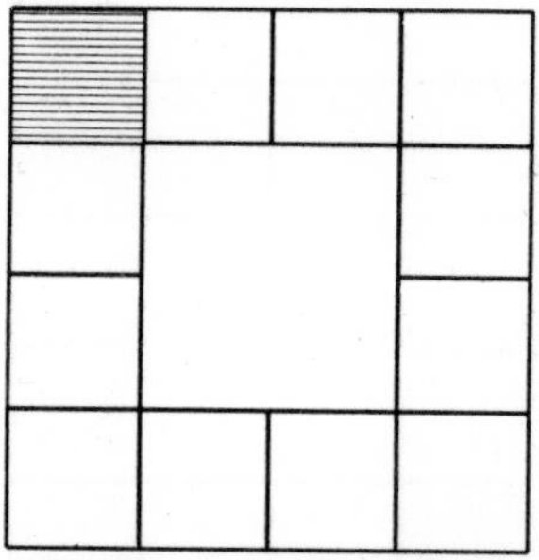

Fig. 30. The shaded box represents Pisces Ascendant.

Pisces: The Pisces-born has a symmetrical middle-sized body. He is virtuous but lacks self-confidence. Though he is reserved, he is a trustworthy friend. He is educated, ambitious, and religious. He will have a good-tempered and virtuous wife.

5

Janma Nakshatras: Determining Personality Traits

The zodiac is marked by 27 equal parts called *Nakshatras* or constellations or asterisms. Each *Nakshatra* forms an arc of $13^1/3$ degrees (13°-20'). Each *Nakshatra* is sub-divided into 4 equal parts called *Padas* or quarters. Each quarter is $3^1/3$ degrees (3°-20'). Thus 2¼ *Nakshatras* (or 9 quarters) comprise a sign. Take for example, the sign Aries which contains 4 quarters of *Ashwini* (13°-20'), 4 of *Bharani* (13°-20'), and 1 of *Krittika* (3°-20'). Again, the remaining 3 quarters of Krittika (10°-0'), 4 of *Rohini* (13°-20'), and 2 of *Mrigashirsha* (6°-40') make up the sign Taurus, and so on.

The *Nakshatra* in which the moon is situated at the time of birth is called the *Janma Nakshatra*. The *Janma Nakshatra* is found by calculating the longitude of the Moon present in a particular sign at the time of birth. For example, if the Moon is in the sign Capricorn with longitude 6°-26' at the time of birth, then the *Janma Nakshatra* would be the 3rd quarter of *Uttarashadha*. The 27 *Nakshatras* can be put into 9 groups of 3 *Nakshatras* each, each group of *Nakshatras* being ruled by a particular planet. The main period *(Dasha)* at birth may be determined by the *Nakshatra* occupied by the Moon at that time.

Nakshatras and their Longitudinal Degrees

Sign	*Nakshatra (Asterism)*	*Padas (Quarters)*	*Longitudinal Degrees*
Aries	1. *Ashwini*	4	13° - 20'
	2. *Bharani*	4	26° - 40'
	3. *Krittika*	1	30° - 0'
Taurus	*Krittika*	3	10° - 0'
	4. *Rohini*	4	23° - 20'
	5. *Mrigashirsha*	2	30° - 0'
Gemini	*Mrigashirsha*	2	6° - 40'
	6. *Ardra*	4	20° - 0'
	7. *Punarvasu*	3	30° - 0'
Cancer	*Punarvasu*	1	3° - 20'
	8. *Pushya*	4	16° - 40'
	9. *Ashlesha*	4	30° - 0'
Leo	10. *Magha*	4	13° - 20'
	11. *Poorvaphalguni*	4	26° - 40'
	12. *Uttaraphalguni*	1	30° - 0'
Virgo	*Uttaraphalguni*	3	10° - 0'
	13. *Hasta*	4	23° - 20'
	14. *Chitra*	2	30° - 0'
Libra	*Chitra*	2	6° - 40'
	15. *Swati*	4	20° - 0'
	16. *Vishakha*	3	30° - 0'
Scorpio	*Vishakha*	1	3° - 20'
	17. *Anuradha*	4	16° - 40'
	18. *Jyeshtha*	4	30° - 0'
Sagittarius	19. *Moola*	4	13° - 20'
	20. *Poorvashadha*	4	26° - 40'
	21. *Uttarashadha*	1	30° - 0'
Capricorn	*Uttarashadha*	3	10° - 0'
	22. *Shravana*	4	23° - 20'
	23. *Dhanishtha*	2	30° - 0'
Aquarius	*Dhanishtha*	2	6° - 40'
	24. *Shatabhishaka*	4	20° - 0'
	25. *Poorvabhadrapada*	3	30° - 0'
Pisces	*Poorvabhadrapada*	1	3° - 20'
	26. *Uttarabhadrapada*	4	16° - 40'
	27. *Revati*	4	30° - 0'

Nakshatras and their Ruling Planets

Nakshatra	*Planet*
Ashwini, Magha, Moola	*Ketu*
Bharani, P.Shadha, P.Phalguni	Venus
Krittika, U.Phalguni, U.Shadha	Sun
Rohini, Hasta, Shravana	Moon
Mrigashira, Chitra, Dhanishtha	Mars
Ardra, Swati, Shatabhisha	*Rahu*
Punarvasu, Vishakha, P.Bhadra	Jupiter
Pushya, Anuradha, U.Bhadra	Saturn
Ashlesha, Jyeshtha, Revati	Mercury

Characteristics of Persons Born under Different *Janma Nakshatras*

The *Janma Nakshatras* have great significance and are considered very important in Indian astrology. They bestow certain characteristics, as given below, on those born under them.

Janma Nakshatra	*Characteristics*
Ashwini	Stubborn, patient, dependable, extravagant
Bharani	Arrogant, careless, faces obstacles
Krittika	Sincere, straightforward, faces many obstacles
Rohini	Sincere, obstinate, extravagant, short-tempered
Mrigashirsha	Sincere, impatient, irritable temperament
Ardra	Selfish, cool-tempered, capable
Punarvasu	Religiously inclined, short-tempered
Pushya	Selfish, inconsistent, nervous temperament
Ashlesha	Insincere, cunning, short-tempered
Magha	Enterprising, soft-spoken, intolerant
Poorvaphalguni	Sweet-spoken, helpful, righteous
Uttaraphalguni	Sincere, reputed, independent, impatient
Hasta	Respectable, generous, faces many ups and downs
Chitra	Courageous, capable, careless

Janma Nakshatra	*Characteristics*
Swati	Adamant, revengeful, independent
Vishakha	Truthful, hard-working, religious
Anuradha	Hard-working, revengeful, faces obstacles
Jyeshtha	Obstinate, hot-tempered, suffers from ill health
Moola	Sincere, extravagant, sweet-natured
Poorvashadha	Religious, argumentative, honest
Uttarashadha	Sincere, well-behaved, soft-spoken
Shravana	Sweet-spoken, capable, God-fearing
Dhanishtha	Trustworthy, capable, argumentative
Shatabhishaka	Truthful, adamant, righteous
Poorva-bhadrapada	Helpful, God-fearing, thrifty
Uttara-bhadrapada	Good speaker, short-tempered, grateful
Revati	Sincere, soft-spoken, stubborn, religious

Harmful *Nakshatra* Quarters

When the Moon is placed in certain quarters or *Padas* of some *Nakshatras*, harmful results, as given below, are obtained:

- The survival of a child should be considered as doubtful if the Moon is in the 1st quarter of *Ashwini*, 4th quarter of *Ashlesha*, 1st quarter of *Magha*, or 4th quarter of *Jyeshtha* at the time of birth.
- If the birth takes place in the 1st quarter of *Moola*, it is harmful to the father; in the 2nd, to the mother; and in the 3rd, it causes loss of money to the parents.
- If the Moon is in the 1st quarter of *Jyeshtha* at the time of birth, it indicates harm to the elder brother; and in the 2nd quarter, to the younger brother.

6

Navamshas: Assessing Planetary Strengths

A *Navamsha* is the most important division of a sign. When a sign is divided into 9 equal parts, each part measuring $3^1/_3$ degrees ($30 \div 9 = 3^1/_3$ or 3° - 20') is called a *Navamsha*. The whole zodiac is divided into 108 *Navamshas*. Thus, each *Navamsha* corresponds to a quarter or *Pada* of a *Nakshatra*.

The *Navamsha* chart is studied to consider the strength of planets. Suppose a planet is debilitated in a *Rashi* but exalted in its *Navamsha* position, it will produce good results. Conversely, if a planet is exalted in a *Rashi* and debilitated in its *Navamsha* position, it is bound to produce unfavourable results. While a *Rashi* chart is only a sketch of the position of the planets, a *Navamsha* chart provides exact information about the position and strength of the planets.

A planet is said to be in *Vargottamamsha* if it occupies the same sign both in the *Rashi* and *Navamsha* charts. The effect of a *Vargottama* planet is comparable with that of a planet situated in its own sign.

The method of calculation of the *Navamsha* position of planets and the *Lagna* has been explained in detail in Chapter 11. The table of *Navamshas* overleaf will facilitate this calculation.

For Aries, Leo, and Sagittarius, *Navamshas* are counted

Navamshas: Divisions of Zodiac Signs

Upto *Deg. Min.*	*Aries* *1*	*Taurus* *2*	*Gemini* *3*	*Cancer* *4*	*Leo* *5*	*Virgo* *6*	*Libra* *7*	*Scorpio* *8*	*Sagitt* *9*	*Capri* *10*	*Aquar* *11*	*Pisces* *12*	*Navamsha*
3 - 20	1	10	7	4	1	10	7	4	1	10	7	4	First
6 - 40	2	11	8	5	2	11	8	5	2	11	8	5	Second
10 - 0	3	12	9	6	3	12	9	6	3	12	9	6	Third
13 - 20	4	1	10	7	4	1	10	7	4	1	10	7	Fourth
16 - 40	5	2	11	8	5	2	11	8	5	2	11	8	Fifth
20 - 0	6	3	12	9	6	3	12	9	6	3	12	9	Sixth
23 - 20	7	4	1	10	7	4	1	10	7	4	1	10	Seventh
26 - 40	8	5	2	11	8	5	2	11	8	5	2	11	Eighth
30 - 0	9	6	3	12	9	6	3	12	9	6	3	12	Ninth

A *Navamsha* is equal to one quarter of a *Nakshatra*.

from Aries to Sagittarius, that is, from sign 1 to sign 9.

For Taurus, Virgo, and Capricorn, *Navamshas* are counted from Capricorn to Virgo, that is, from sign 10 to sign 6.

For Gemini, Libra, and Aquarius, *Navamshas* are counted from Libra to Gemini, that is, from sign 7 to sign 3.

For Cancer, Scorpio, and Pisces, *Navamshas* are counted from Cancer to Pisces, that is, from sign 4 to sign 12.

Take, for example, Aries and divide it into 9 equal parts. The 1st *Navamsha* is of Aries itself, the 2nd of Taurus, the 3rd of Gemini, and so on. Now divide Taurus into 9 equal parts. The 1st *Navamsha* is of Capricorn, the 2nd is of Aquarius, the 3rd of Pisces, and so on.

A *Navamsha* chart is examined in a similar manner as a *Rashi* chart, except that planets do not exercise their aspects in the *Navamsha* chart as they do in the *Rashi* chart. Planets occupying friendly or exalted signs in a *Navamsha* chart produce benefic results, while planets in inimical or debilitated signs produce malefic results.

Characteristics of Persons Born in Different *Navamshas* Occupied by the Moon

Aries	Cruel, wealthy, thieving tendency, potential to be a good military officer, restless mind
Taurus	Broad face and shoulders, big belly, intelligent
Gemini	Good-looking, fickle, religious, learned, writing skills
Cancer	Irritable, wealthy, crooked eyes
Leo	Projecting nose, strong body, proud and renowned
Virgo	Good-looking, lean body, sweet speech
Libra	Sensual, attractive eyes, lean body, miserly
Scorpio	Lean body, miserable, sickly, intelligent, cruel
Sagittarius	Wealthy, virtuous, lazy
Capricorn	Greedy, fickle, sensuous, cruel
Aquarius	Miserable, deceitful, fickle
Pisces	Slender body, sensuous, wealthy, learned

Characteristics of Persons Born in Different *Navamshas* Occupied by the Ascendant

Aries or Scorpio	Restless, wavering mind, greedy, cruel
Taurus or Libra	Popular, learned, sensuous
Gemini or Virgo	Capable, famous, learned, slender body
Cancer	Learned, wealthy, will enjoy worldly pleasures
Leo	Strong, wealthy, lustful, cruel
Sagittarius or Pisces	Happy, learned, will occupy good position
Capricorn or Aquarius	Poor, unhappy, short-tempered

7

The Influence of Planets

Each sign of the zodiac is governed by a planet which is said to be its owner or lord or ruling planet.

Signs and Their Ruling Planets

The Moon is the owner or ruling planet of the sign Cancer, and the Sun, of the sign Leo. All other planets rule over two signs each. The signs that they rule over are called their own signs or houses. Aries and Scorpio are ruled by Mars, Taurus and Libra by Venus, Gemini and Virgo by Mercury, Sagittarius and Pisces by Jupiter, Capricorn and Aquarius by Saturn. There is no unanimity regarding the signs ruled by *Rahu* and *Ketu.* According to Western astrology, Uranus rules over Aquarius, and Neptune over Pisces. The planets, in their own signs, are strong.

Signs	*Ruling Planet (Lord)*
Leo	Sun
Cancer	Moon
Aries, Scorpio	Mars
Gemini, Virgo	Mercury
Sagittarius, Pisces	Jupiter
Taurus, Libra	Venus
Capricorn, Aquarius	Saturn

Exalted, Debilitated and *Moolatrikona* Signs of Planets: The places where planets attain their full power are called exalted or *Uchcha* signs. The Sun is said to be exalted in Aries, the Moon in Taurus, Mars in Capricorn, Mercury in Virgo, Jupiter in Cancer, Venus in Pisces, and Saturn in Libra. Exalted planets are considered to be very powerful. Each planet has a particular degree which is termed as its highest exaltation point. For example, if the Sun is at 10° of Aries in a horoscope, it is considered to be an exalted planet.

Planet	*Exalted in (Uchcha)*	*Strong in (Moolatrikona)*	*Debilitated in (Neecha)*
Sun	Aries	Leo	Libra
Moon	Taurus	Taurus	Scorpio
Mars	Capricorn	Aries	Cancer
Mercury	Virgo	Virgo	Pisces
Jupiter	Cancer	Sagittarius	Capricorn
Venus	Pisces	Libra	Virgo
Saturn	Libra	Aquarius	Aries

The 7th sign from the exaltation sign of the planet is called its debilitated or *Neecha* sign. The debilitation sign for the Sun, for example, is Libra, as it is the 7th sign from Aries and its lowest debilitation point is at 10°. The planet in its debilitated sign is considered to be weak.

Certain strong positions called *Moolatrikonas* are similar to those of exaltation. The Sun's *Moolatrikona* is Leo, the Moon's is Taurus, Mercury's is Virgo, and so on.

Planet	*Exaltation/ Debilitation Degrees*	*Moolatrikona Degrees*
Sun	10°	0 - 20°
Moon	3°	4 - 20°
Mars	28°	0 - 12°
Mercury	15°	16 - 20°
Jupiter	5°	0 - 10°
Venus	27°	0 - 15°
Saturn	20°	0 - 20°

Benefic and Malefic Planets

The good or benefic planets by nature are Jupiter, Venus, the waxing Moon, and a well-associated Mercury.

The evil or malefic planets by nature are the Sun, Mars, Saturn, the waning Moon, *Rahu*, *Ketu*, and a badly-associated Mercury.

The Moon is considered strong between the 11th day of the bright fortnight *(Shukla Paksha Ekadashi)*, and the 5th day of the dark fortnight *(Krishna Paksha Panchami)* of the lunar month.

By nature, Mercury is considered to be a benefic planet. But in itself its positive qualities are so weak that it may be better classified as indifferent — neither benefic nor malefic. It becomes benefic or malefic only by association. If it is associated with the waning Moon, the Sun, Mars, or Saturn, it is considered as malefic. When associated with the waxing Moon, Jupiter, or Venus, it is considered as benefic.

Inter-Planetary Relationships

Due to their inherent nature, the planets are friendly with certain planets and inimical to others. There are two kinds of friendship — permanent and temporary. The natural permanent disposition of planets towards each other is shown in the following Table.

Planets become temporary friends with others by virtue of their sign positions. The planets found in the 2nd, 3rd, 4th, 10th, 11th, and 12th signs from any other planet become its temporary friends. Those in the remaining signs become temporary enemies. Both types of relationships should be considered while reading a horoscope, and interpretations made as given below:

Permanent friend	+ Temporary friend	= Best friend
Permanent friend	+ Temporary enemy	= Neutral
Permanent enemy	+ Temporary enemy	= Bitter enemy
Permanent enemy	+ Temporary friend	= Neutral
Permanent neutral	+ Temporary friend	= Friend
Permanent neutral	+ Temporary enemy	= Enemy

Planet	*Friends*	*Neutrals*	*Enemies*
Sun	Moon, Mars, Jupiter	Mercury	Venus, Saturn
Moon	Sun, Mercury	Mars, Jupiter, Venus, Saturn	None
Mars	Sun, Moon, Jupiter	Venus, Saturn	Mercury
Mercury	Sun, Venus	Mars, Jupiter, Saturn	Moon
Jupiter	Sun, Moon, Mars	Saturn	Mercury, Venus
Venus	Mercury, Saturn	Mars, Jupiter	Sun, Moon
Saturn	Mercury, Venus	Jupiter	Sun, Mars, Moon
Rahu & *Ketu*	Mercury, Venus, Saturn	Jupiter	Sun, Mars, Moon

Planetary Aspects

The manner in which a planet looks at a house (and the planets therein) from its position is termed an aspect. Under the Indian system all planets aspect the 7th house (and planets therein) from the house occupied by them. However Mars, Jupiter, and Saturn have special aspects besides their 7th house aspect.

Planet	*House Aspected*
Sun	7th
Moon	7th
Mars	4th, 7th, 8th
Mercury	7th
Jupiter	5th, 7th, 9th
Venus	7th
Saturn	3rd, 7th, 10th
Rahu	5th, 7th, 9th
Ketu	5th, 7th, 9th

Mars, Jupiter, and Saturn have other aspects which exert a more powerful influence than the 7th house aspect. Jupiter aspects the 5th and 9th houses from the house occupied by him. The 5th house aspect, as per the Western system, is a trine aspect and is always considered good.

Mars aspects the 4th and 8th houses. The 4th aspect as per Western astrology, is a square aspect, and is considered bad. The 8th house aspect is not that bad and is somewhat relieving in nature.

Saturn aspects the 3rd and 10th houses. The 3rd house aspect is a sextile aspect which, according to the Western system, is good. However, under the Indian system, the aspecting planet being evil, all its aspects are considered as evil.

Rahu and *Ketu* aspect the 5th and 9th houses apart from the 7th.

In Western astrology there are two important types of aspects which can be divided into benefic and malefic. The benefic aspects are sextile (⚹) and trine (△); the malefic aspects are squares (□) and opposition (☍).

Sextile: This aspect is caused when one planet is in the 3rd place from the other, that is, 60° apart. This aspect is always considered good.

Trine: When a planet is in the 5th place from the other, that is, 120° apart, this aspect is also considered good.

Square: When a planet is in the 4th place from the other, that is, 90° apart, this aspect is deemed to be evil.

Opposition: When a planet is in the 7th place from the other, that is, 180° apart, this aspect is also deemed to be evil.

Planetary Strengths

Planets have their own strengths as well as those bestowed on them by virtue of their position, time, and motion.

Positional Strength *(Sthanabala)*: A planet acquires positional strength when it occupies its own, exaltation,

Planetary Features

Planets	*Dispositions*	*Directions*	*Sex*	*Colours*	*Gems*
The Sun	*Satvika*	East	Male	Copper	Ruby
The Moon	*Satvika*	North-west	Female	White	Pearl
Mars	*Tamasika*	South	Male	Blood-red	Coral
Mercury	*Rajasika*	North	Eunuch	Green	Emerald
Jupiter	*Satvika*	North-east	Male	Yellow	Topaz
Venus	*Rajasika*	South-east	Female	Mixture of all colours	Diamond
Saturn	*Tamasika*	West	Eunuch	Black	Sapphire
Rahu	*Tamasika*	South-west	Female	Black	Agate
Ketu	*Tamasika*	South-west	Eunuch	Brown	Cat's eye

Moolatrikona, or *Navamsha* sign, or a sign owned by its friend. For example, if the Sun occupies his own sign Leo or his sign of exaltation (Aries), he is considered to be positionally strong.

Directional Strength *(Digabala)*: Jupiter and Mercury are considered to be strong in the East (ascendant), the Sun and Mars in the South (10th house), Saturn in the West (7th house), and the Moon and Venus in the North (4th house).

Natural Strength *(Naisargikabala)*: Each planet has a natural strength, irrespective of its position. The Sun is considered to be the most powerful planet, followed by the Moon, Venus, Jupiter, Mercury, Mars, and Saturn.

Temporal Strength *(Kalabala)*: The Sun, Jupiter, and Venus are considered powerful if the birth takes place during the day. The Moon, Mars, and Saturn are considered powerful if the birth takes place at night. Mercury is considered powerful both during the day and night.

The benefic planets are considered powerful during the bright fortnight, while the malefics are deemed strong during the dark fortnight of the lunar month.

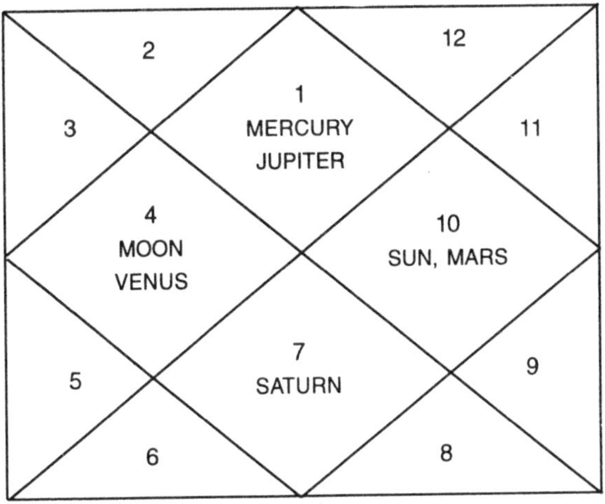

Fig. 31. The houses in which certain planets are strong

Motional Strength *(Cheshtabala)*: The Sun and Moon acquire motional strength when moving in the Northern course *(Uttarayana)*, that is, when posited in the signs Capricorn, Aquarius, Pisces, Aries, Taurus, or Gemini. The remaining five planets gain motional strength when they are in retrograde motion, or when in conjunction with the Moon.

There are certain other rules which should be considered while judging the strength of planets in a horoscope.

1. A planet has its full strength in its exaltation *(Uchcha)* sign.
2. A planet has three-fourths of its full strength in its *Moolatrikona* sign.
3. A planet has half its full strength in its own sign.
4. A planet has one-fourth of its full strength in its friendly sign.
5. A planet has less than one-fourth of its strength in an inimical sign.
6. A planet has zero strength in its debilitated *(Neecha)* sign, or when it is combust with the Sun.
7. A planet that owns both a quadrant and a trine is

called *Yogakaraka*. A *Yogakaraka* planet is considered to be very strong.

8. A benefic planet occupying a quadrant *(Kendra)* is considered very good.
9. A malefic planet that owns a *Kendra* is considered very good.
10. A benefic planet produces good results in its exaltation sign, while a malefic planet is good in a debilitated sign.
11. A planet which is debilitated in a *Rashi* chart but exalted in a *Navamsha* chart is considered strong.
12. A planet in retrograde motion is strong when debilitated, and weak when exalted. Another view is that benefic planets in a retrograde position bestow power and wealth, while malefics in the same condition cause evil and loss.

Favourable Planets for Each Ascendant

Planets become favourable or capable of producing good results for an individual when they own at least one of the quadrants *(Kendra)* or trines *(Trikona)*. However, a planet owning the 7th house (a quadrant) is always unfavourable.

Ascendant	*Favourable Planets*
Aries	Sun, Moon, Mars, Jupiter, Saturn
Taurus	Sun, Mercury, Venus, Saturn*
Gemini	Mercury, Venus, Saturn
Cancer	Moon, Mars*, Jupiter
Leo	Sun, Mars*, Jupiter
Virgo	Mercury, Venus, Saturn
Libra	Moon, Mercury, Venus, Saturn*
Scorpio	Sun, Moon, Mars, Jupiter, Saturn
Sagittarius	Sun, Mars, Jupiter
Capricorn	Mars, Mercury, Venus*, Saturn
Aquarius	Mars, Mercury, Venus*, Saturn
Pisces	Moon, Mars, Jupiter

* *Yogakaraka* planets.

8

Ruling Planets: Shaping Life & Events

Each planet is a significator *(Karaka)* or promoter of certain traits and matters associated with an individual. The planet itself is personified as being the possessor of several characteristics and having a significant influence over specified spheres in an individual's life.

For example, the Moon signifies the mother, Mars signifies brothers, and so on. When a significator is well-placed in a horoscope, it generally promotes matters and events signified by it.

The Sun: The Sun has a strong, square-built body with sparse hair. He has a dark-brown hue, matched with a fiery, daring, wrathful, and bilious temperament.

The Sun rules over the Eastern direction. He is strong during the daytime and the dark half of the lunar month.

The Sun signifies the father, soul, will-power, influence, position, health, energy, and courage.

The parts of the body which are controlled by him are the bones, head, stomach, heart, eyes, brain, throat, and spleen. The diseases signified by the Sun are high fever, blood pressure, eye troubles, cerebral disorders, and afflictions of the throat, ear, and nose.

The Moon: The Moon is round in shape and white in

colour. She has a large body, complemented with a cold, mild temperament and sweet speech. She is phlegmatic and windy.

The Moon rules over the North-west. She is strong during the night and the bright half of the lunar month.

The Moon signifies the mother, face, mind, blood, intelligence, beauty, and vital energy.

The organs of the body ruled by the Moon are the nerves, arteries, brain, stomach, uterus, bladder, breast, ovaries, and sex organs. The diseases associated with her are catarrh, jaundice, hysteria, dysentery, dyspepsia, asthma, bronchitis, skin, and venereal diseases.

Mars: Mars can be described as possessing a youthful appearance, curly hair, lean body, and slender waist. He is red in colour, rash in action, fickle-minded and cruel, but generous. He has a bilious temperament.

Mars rules over the Southern direction. He is strong during the night and the dark half of the lunar month.

Mars signifies strength, brothers, conspiracy, sports, games, surgery, mechanical work, scandals, army, lands, mines, minerals, and wounds.

The parts of the body associated with him are the bone marrow, bile, eyes, limbs, and urinary system. The ailments denoted by Mars are high fever, cuts and burns, decomposition of the marrow, haemorrhage, abortion, and menstrual disorders.

Mercury: Mercury is lean-bodied and green in colour. Its nature is a mixture of three humours — bile, phlegm, and wind. Mercury is intelligent, learned, and fun-loving. It is talkative but stammers while speaking.

Mercury rules over the North. It is powerful both during the day and the night.

Mercury is the significator of an individual's profession, education, speech, intellect, communications of every kind, poetry, writing, commerce, advertising, journalism, and transport.

The parts of the body ruled by Mercury are the skin, brain, nervous system, nose, thorax, and tongue. The disorders signified by Mercury include dumbness, mental disorders, and skin diseases.

Jupiter: Jupiter boasts a corpulent body, golden colour, and brown hair. He is noble, wise, and phlegmatic.

Jupiter is the lord of the North-eastern direction, and is powerful during the day and the bright half of the lunar month.

The areas signified by Jupiter are business, children, wealth, fame, wisdom, legal affairs, and banks.

Jupiter rules over the feet, stomach, intestines, and ears. The disorders caused by Jupiter are liver and digestive complaints, dropsy, flatulence, abscessess, and appendicitis.

Venus: Venus personifies a large and beautiful body, black curly hair, broad lovely eyes, and a fair complexion. She is soft in speech and is pleasure loving. Her disposition is windy and phlegmatic.

Venus rules over the South-east and is strong during the day and the bright fortnight.

Venus governs love, courtship, marriage, art, music, dancing, decoration, vehicles, luxury articles, trade, industry, and chemicals.

She exercises control over the sexual organs, semen, urine, face, and hair. She causes venereal complaints, sexual weakness, spermatorrhoea, leucorrhoea, eye and nose troubles.

Saturn: Saturn is dark, lame, and lazy. Its body is lean, the eyes sunken, nails thick, teeth protruding, and limbs and hair stiff. Saturn is dirty, foolish, cruel, and windy in nature.

Saturn governs the Western direction. It is powerful during the night and the dark fortnight.

It denotes an evil nature and is the significator of longevity, concentration, sorrow, impediments, gardening and farming, mining, property, and real estate.

The parts of the body ruled by Saturn are the muscles, bladder, excretory system, and teeth. The ailments caused by Saturn are toothache, asthma, tuberculosis, rheumatism, and paralysis.

Uranus: Uranus signifies inventions, research, electronics, occultism, astrology, photography, aviation, and intense mental activity.

Neptune: Neptune is the significator of sea travel, sensuous pleasures, spiritual experiences, and higher forms of music and art.

Note: Uranus and Neptune find no place in Indian astrology as mentioned in Chapter 7.

Rahu: *Rahu* is tall, dirty, and black in colour. She always speaks ill of others and is the lord of the South-west.

Rahu signifies maternal relations, skin diseases, accidents, intrigues, and foreign travels. The diseases caused by *Rahu* are epilepsy, small pox, leprosy, tuberculosis, malaria, and itches.

Ketu: *Ketu* is also tall and dark in colour, and is fiery and harsh in speech.

Ketu is the significator of paternal relations, skin diseases, sinful acts, foreign languages, and foreign travels. The diseases caused by *Ketu* are measles, small pox, itches, and leprosy.

Planet	*Significator (Karaka) of*
Sun	Father, influence, energy
Moon	Mother, mind, face
Mars	Brothers, strength, mechanical work
Mercury	Profession, education, speech
Jupiter	Children, wealth, fame
Venus	Marriage, courtship, pleasures
Saturn	Longevity, sorrow, impediments
Uranus	Astrology, electronics, research
Neptune	Spiritual and sensuous experiences
Rahu	Maternal relations
Ketu	Paternal relations

9

Planets & Zodiac Signs: Favourable and Unfavourable Relationships

A planet can occupy any one of the twelve signs or *Rashis* in a horoscope. However, it does not promote similar results in all signs. It bestows favourable results in certain signs, has unfavourable effects in others, and remains neutral in still others. This is due to the fact that:

- A planet has either a natural friendship or enmity with other planets. The Moon, for example, is a natural friend of the Sun and Mercury. The signs owned by the Sun and Mercury are Leo, Gemini, and Virgo, respectively. Therefore, the Moon will bestow favourable results in those signs whose lords are friendly with her.
- The Moon herself owns the sign Cancer and is in an exalted position in Taurus. Therefore, both Cancer and Taurus are also favourable to the Moon.

The Moon: When planets are posited in different signs, the characteristics of individuals are influenced by them. The favourable signs for the Moon are: Taurus, Gemini, Cancer, Leo, and Virgo.

Zodiac Sign	*Influence of the Moon*
Aries	Round eyes, sparse hair, bruises on the head, ambitious, lustful, irritable, fickle-minded
Taurus	Broad chest, curly hair, handsome, popular, respectable, generous, successful, romantic, happy in middle and old age
Gemini	Projecting nose, black eyes, curly hair, tall, passionate, intelligent, learned, sweet-spoken
Cancer	Short-statured, charming, wealthy, emotional, happy, intelligent
Leo	Broad face, reddish eyes, strong body, bold, proud, charitable, unhappy
Virgo	Attractive, modest, reserved, honest, long-armed, drooping shoulders, sweet speech, intelligent, fond of pleasure and the opposite sex
Libra	Tall, lean, deformed limbs, intelligent, learned, religious, amicable, lover of pleasure and the opposite sex
Scorpio	Broad eyes, wide chest, well-formed body, mischievous, undependable, straightforward, greedy, wealthy
Sagittarius	Oval face, long neck, happy, liberal, influential, popular, soft-spoken
Capricorn	Thin body and face, clever, crafty, low morals
Aquarius	Tall, well-formed body, sensual, diplomatic, courteous
Pisces	Projecting nose, symmetrical body, soft-spoken, religious, charitable, learned, fond of the opposite sex

The Sun: The favourable signs for the Sun are: Aries, Cancer, Leo, Scorpio, Sagittarius, and Pisces.

Zodiac Sign	*Influence of the Sun*
Aries	Strong and well-built, aggressive, popular, ambitious, courageous, intelligent
Taurus	Prominent nose, intelligent, tactful, sociable
Gemini	Well-proportioned body, learned, wealthy, polite, intelligent, interested in science/mathematics
Cancer	Lustful, poor, drunkard, fickle
Leo	Physically strong, traveller, poor, obstinate, happy-go-lucky
Virgo	Effeminate, soft-spoken, interested in intellectual pursuits
Libra	Well-built body, fickle, mean, obstinate, prone to committing bad deeds
Scorpio	Strong body, bold, cruel, unprincipled, possessing surgical skill
Sagittarius	Tall, well-proportioned body, wealthy, happy, intelligent, religious, short-tempered
Capricorn	Thin, small body, stupid, poor, timid, mean, unhappy
Aquarius	Medium height, poor, base, unfortunate, lustful
Pisces	Short-statured, rich, religious, learned, loved by the opposite sex

Mars: The favourable signs for Mars are: Aries, Cancer, Leo, Scorpio, Sagittarius, and Capricorn.

Zodiac Sign	*Influence of Mars*
Aries	Prominent position in military, police or business, rich, happy, sensual, generous
Taurus	Immoral, timid, harsh-tongued, unhappy
Gemini	Intelligent, skilled in music, learned, unhappy
Cancer	Wealthy, intelligent, destined to travel abroad, wicked, possessing weak eyesight
Leo	Poor, successful, unhappy domestic

Zodiac Sign	Influence of Mars
	circumstances, interested in astrology, mathematics
Virgo	Respectable, affluent, sensuous, extravagant, charming, revengeful
Libra	Materialistic, immoral, boastful, deformities in body, quarrelsome
Scorpio	Clever, proud, materialistic, diplomatic, passionate
Sagittarius	Famous, holding good position, possessing many enemies
Capricorn	Wealthy, very good status, bold, generous, influential
Aquarius	Poor, untruthful, unlucky, unhappy
Pisces	Restless, possessing many enemies, passionate, unprincipled

Mercury: The favourable signs for Mercury are: Taurus, Gemini, Leo, Virgo, and Libra.

Zodiac Sign	Influence of Mercury
Aries	Lean-built, wicked, unscrupulous, deceitful
Taurus	Well-built, high position, respectable, moneyed, sensual
Gemini	Sweet-spoken, studious, rich, tactful
Cancer	Rich, lover of music, sensual, hostile to close relatives
Leo	Poor, boastful, unhappy, wanderer
Virgo	Learned, respectable, religious, potential to be an author, generous
Libra	Courteous, sociable, philosophical, materialistic, spendthrift
Scorpio	Stupid, miser, selfish, reckless
Sagittarius	Well-built, virtuous, learned, generous, intelligent
Capricorn	Miserable, liar, fickle, wicked
Aquarius	Poor, quarrelsome, unlucky, unhappy, scholarly
Pisces	Devoid of learning, wealth and sons, lover of the opposite sex

Jupiter: The favourable signs for Jupiter are: Aries, Cancer, Leo, Scorpio, Sagittarius, and Pisces

Zodiac Sign	*Influence of Jupiter*
Aries	Wealthy, liberal, bold, intelligent, famous, good status, happy
Taurus	Wealthy, liberal, popular, polite, happy
Gemini	Happy, religious, oratorial skills, learned, creative ability
Cancer	Wealthy, influential, intelligent, famous, respectable, learned, happy
Leo	Active, brave, ambitious, happy, intelligent
Virgo	Intelligent, ambitious, affluent, learned, selfish
Libra	Intelligent, religious, attractive, pleasant
Scorpio	Proud, zealous, sick, selfish, unhappy
Sagittarius	Rich, generous, intelligent, influential, status
Capricorn	Base, poor, unhappy, tactless, generous
Aquarius	Greedy, sick, popular, sympathetic, learned, lacking in wealth
Pisces	Respectable, bold, wealthy, good position

Venus: The favourable signs for Venus are: Taurus, Gemini, Virgo, Libra, Capricorn, Aquarius, and Pisces.

Zodiac Sign	*Influence of Venus*
Aries	Immoral, easygoing, extravagant, unhappy
Taurus	Popular, rich, handsome, sensuous
Gemini	Wealthy, intelligent, sensuous, skilled in arts
Cancer	Arrogant, intelligent, unhappy, sensuous
Leo	Licentious, procuring money through women, miserable due to his own acts
Virgo	Rich, clever, unhappy, lustful
Libra	Intelligent, generous, respectable, sensuous, destined to travel widely
Scorpio	Querulous, proud, lacking in wealth
Sagittarius	Powerful, rich, respectable, happy, high position
Capricorn	Weak, learned, immoral, unhappy, poor
Aquarius	Popular, respectable, timid, helpful
Pisces	Wealthy, learned, charitable, liked by all

Saturn: The favourable signs for Saturn are: Taurus, Gemini, Virgo, Libra, Capricorn, and Aquarius

Zodiac Sign	*Influence of Saturn*
Aries	Foolish, deceitful, poor, wanderer, quarrelsome
Taurus	Successful, lustful, clever, lacking in wealth
Gemini	Unhappy, poor, lazy, wanderer, ingenious
Cancer	Stubborn, sick, cunning, not rich
Leo	Mean, unhappy, angry temperament, writer
Virgo	Weak constitution, poor, immoral, quarrelsome
Libra	Tall, tactful, famous, wealthy, respectable, lustful
Scorpio	Fickle, arrogant, unhappy, weak health
Sagittarius	Learned, wealthy, famous, happy during the last part of his life
Capricorn	Wealthy, intelligent, peevish, selfish, good status
Aquarius	Diplomatic, happy, practical, intelligent, wealthy
Pisces	Rich, polite, happy, clever, helping nature

Uranus: Uranus was identified as a planet in 1781 by William Herschel. It has completed only two revolutions round the Sun since its discovery. Uranus exerts its greatest influence in the sign Aquarius and, therefore, this sign may be termed as its 'house'.

Zodiac Sign	*Influence of Uranus*
Aries	Tall, lean and strong constitution, quick to anger, ambitious
Taurus	Short, thickset person, passionate, revengeful, conceited
Gemini	Tall, thin stature, generous, good-natured
Cancer	Short, corpulent person, violent, conceited, eccentric
Leo	Tall stature, strong shoulders, proud, generous disposition
Virgo	Short stature, lean body, studious, mean

Zodiac Sign	*Influence of Uranus*
Libra	Tall stature, strong body, ambitious, quick temper
Scorpio	Short and thickset body, deceitful, cunning
Sagittarius	Tall stature, generous and independent disposition
Capricorn	Medium height, proud, conceited
Aquarius	Medium height, ingenious, pleasant disposition
Pisces	Medium height, sickly, dejected and dull

Neptune and Pluto: Neptune was discovered in 1846 and Pluto in 1930. Their movement is extremely slow. Hence it will be many years before reliable information as to the kind of persons produced by them in the various signs can be ascertained. Neptune exerts its greatest influence in the sign Pisces, and Pluto in the sign Scorpio. They may, therefore, be termed as their 'houses'.

As generally understood, the disposition effected by Neptune is that of an intuitional, impulsive, restless, doubtful, ambitious, and sensual person, inclined towards spiritualism and occultism. Pluto indicates an impulsive, stubborn, and violent nature.

***Rahu* and *Ketu*:** There is much difference of opinion about the favourable signs of the two nodes — *Rahu* and *Ketu*. They are considered benefic when they are in the signs owned by benefic planets or are in the company of benefic planets. They are considered harmful when they are in the signs owned by malefic planets or are in the company of malefic planets. When alone, they act like Saturn and Mars, respectively.

10

Planetary Effects on Houses

Each house of a horoscope indicates or signifies several matters which have been explained in Chapter 3. A house is also represented by one or more planets which are called significators or *Karakas* of that house. The significators of different houses are given in Fig. 32.

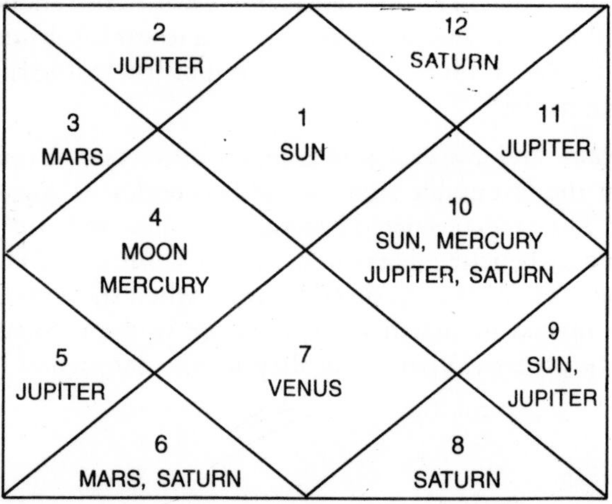

Fig. 32. Houses and the planets which are their significators

When the lords of several houses and their respective significators are related with each other either through conjunction[1] or aspect, they bestow positive effects on the native concerned. Some planets, however, do not yield good results if posited in the houses of which they are the significators. Mars in the 3rd, Mercury in the 4th, Jupiter in the 5th, and Venus in the 7th do not produce good results. However, Jupiter in the 2nd and Saturn in the 8th house increase wealth and longevity, respectively.

Planetary Effects on the Houses

The effects that the nine planets, as well as *Rahu* and *Ketu* have on the twelve houses are given below:

The Sun:

1st House	Healthy, proud, prosperous, daring, obstinate, lazy
2nd House	Good income but loss of money, stubborn, a facial disease, stammering
3rd House	Bold, prosperous, famous, hot-tempered
4th House	Intelligent, reputed, but devoid of happiness, comforts, and house
5th House	Poor, intelligent, unhappy, few children
6th House	Bold, successful, wealthy, tactful
7th House	Some trouble in married life, humiliated by women, impatient, irreligious
8th House	Eye troubles, few issues, loss of money, ill health, sudden gains
9th House	Wealth, children and happiness, friction with father, lucky, successful
10th House	Endowed with status, fame, power, health and children
11th House	Learned, wealthy, long life, success, status
12th House	Defective eyes, poor, base, no happiness from children

1. When two planets are in the same sign and approximately in the same longitude.

The Moon:

1st House	Modest, fickle, romantic, easygoing, obstinate
2nd House	Rich, soft-spoken, charming, intelligent, large family
3rd House	Cruel, unscrupulous, miserly, sickly
4th House	Happy, well-educated, blessed with fame and friends, owning vehicles, sensuous
5th House	Good wife, children and position
6th House	Idler, poor, stomach complaints, many enemies, servile to the fair sex
7th House	Passionate, zealous, fond of the opposite sex, successful
8th House	Fickle-minded, few children, ill health, early death of mother
9th House	Popular, wealthy, religious, successful, good reputation and children
10th House	Wealthy, popular, intelligent, good status, passionate
11th House	Longevity, wealthy, learned, many children and friends, good status
12th House	Miserable, lazy, wicked, eye complaints or defect in some limb

Mars:

1st House	Adventurous, strong, hot-tempered, cruel, fickle, possessing marks of injuries
2nd House	Harsh-tongued, wicked, unpopular, devoid of learning and money
3rd House	Intelligent, courageous, unpopular, few brothers
4th House	Loss of mother, friends, happiness and comforts, quarrelsome
5th House	Loss of happiness and sons, cruel, unprincipled
6th House	Wealthy, powerful, lazy, lustful, mean, successful against enemies
7th House	Unhappy married life, passionate, unsuccessful
8th House	Poor, no marriage, short life
9th House	Cruel, stubborn, loss of father
10th House	Popular, clever, healthy, famous and powerful

11th House	Learned, wealthy, happy, influential
12th House	Defective eyesight, cruel, unsuccessful, poor

Mercury:

1st House	Learned, intellectual, clever, polite
2nd House	Wealthy, intelligent, clever, many children
3rd House	Clever, cruel, tactful, diplomatic
4th House	Intelligent, learned, happy and wealthy
5th House	Learned, showy, quarrelsome, many issues, respectable
6th House	Quarrelsome, showy, respectable, breaks in education
7th House	Literary ability, skilful, diplomatic, successful
8th House	Wealthy, few issues, ill health, longevity
9th House	Highly educated, intelligent, many children, wealthy, popular
10th House	Rich, happy, intelligent, charitable
11th House	Wealthy, happy, successful in business, long life
12th House	Intelligent, worried, lustful, spendthrift, few children

Jupiter:

1st House	Learned, highly educated, blessed with children and long life, influential leader
2nd House	Blessed with a good partner, prosperity, learning and eloquence
3rd House	Unscrupulous, miserly, many brothers, famous
4th House	Well-educated, wealthy, happy, several modes of conveyance
5th House	Intelligent, good status
6th House	Intelligent, devoid of enemies, unlucky
7th House	Educated, good partner, sons, diplomatic
8th House	Long life, poor, learned, unhappy
9th House	Famous, high position, devout and philosophical, many children
10th House	Renowned, wealthy, ambitious, virtuous
11th House	Very wealthy, long life, influential, philanthropic
12th House	Unlucky, sinful, wicked, devoid of children, money and happiness

Venus:

1st House	Attractive personality, fortunate, bold, happy, amorous, successful, practical, long life
2nd House	Attractive face, happy, wealthy, educated, literary skill, sweet speech, large family
3rd House	Affluent, miserly
4th House	Happy, educated, blessed with children and affectionate mother, popular
5th House	Prosperous, intelligent, good status, many daughters, educated
6th House	Poor, sickly, issueless, no enemies, licentious
7th House	Querulous, lustful, unhappy married life
8th House	Famous, sickly, unexpected gains
9th House	Fortunate, endowed with sons and friends, religious, comfortable life
10th House	Famous, good status, popular
11th House	Rich, intelligent, influential, popular
12th House	Wealthy, miserly, sexually active, weak eyesight

Saturn:

1st House	Dirty, lazy, unscrupulous, cunning, sickly
2nd House	Diseased face, breaks in education, little wealth, weak eyesight, harsh-tongued
3rd House	Intelligent, bold, generous, wicked
4th House	Unhappy, devoid of mother, house and vehicle, interrupted education
5th House	Loss of wealth, happiness and children, wicked
6th House	Stubborn, clever, deaf, few children
7th House	Mean, fickle, diplomatic, unhappy married life
8th House	Poor, fickle, clever, few children
9th House	Devoid of wealth, father and children, wicked, diplomatic
10th House	Wealthy, famous, happy, intelligent, sudden rise and fall in position
11th House	Long life, affluent, influential, learned, interrupted education
12th House	Unpopular, poor, unhappy, many enemies, extravagant

Uranus:

1st House	Stubborn, conceited, proud, impulsive
2nd House	Sudden gains and sudden losses
3rd House	Skills of creative thinking, writing and inventions, strained relations with brothers and sisters
4th House	Estranged from parents, trouble with money or property
5th House	Bad influence on children, love affairs
6th House	Ill health and troubles from enemies
7th House	Unhappy marriage, illicit relationships with women, ill-suited for business or partnership
8th House	Wife/husband poor, fatal accident
9th House	Fond of occult sciences, astrology, arts and sciences, sudden foreign travel
10th House	Leadership qualities — both creditable and discreditable, dispute with superiors
11th House	Has undependable friends
12th House	Many secret enemies

Neptune:

1st House	Short temper, imaginative and dreamy, inclined towards spiritualism
2nd House	Easy money, fear of poverty
3rd House	Courageous
4th House	Loss of property, wealth or happiness
5th House	Disappointment in love and from children, fondness for pleasure
6th House	Ill health, many enemies
7th House	Dramatic and artistic ability, illicit relationships with the opposite sex, unfortunate marriage
8th House	Interest in spiritualism, fatal accident
9th House	Unethical, success in publishing and travelling, inclination towards occult studies
10th House	Unprincipled, job-hopper, worries
11th House	Annoyances from friends
12th House	Fear of enemies

Rahu:

1st House	Affable at times, cruel at other times, irreligious, sickly
2nd House	Diseased face, peevish, hostile, stammering defect
3rd House	Wealthy, courageous, powerful
4th House	Hostile, source of annoyance to others
5th House	Issueless, poor, stomach complaints, kind, timid
6th House	Long life, affluent, happy, no enemies
7th House	Sickly, arrogant, poor, adulterer
8th House	Short life, lazy, sickly, quarrelsome
9th House	Renowned, irreligious, leader
10th House	Intelligent, arrogant, famous
11th House	Wealthy, long life, learned, ear disease
12th House	Extravagant, impolite

Ketu:

1st House	Sickly, miserly, unhappy
2nd House	Devoid of learning and wealth, harsh speech
3rd House	Wealthy, famous, adventurous, moral
4th House	Quarrelsome, devoid of happiness and comforts, finds faults in others
5th House	Sickly, stupid, loss of children
6th House	Learned, famous, generous, popular
7th House	Stupid, lazy, wanderer, may prove dangerous for life partner who is a shrew
8th House	Miserly, sickly, licentious
9th House	Angry, irreligious, indolent, arrogant, friction with father
10th House	Learned, happy, religious, popular
11th House	Respectable, wealthy, intelligent, moralist
12th House	Shameless, committing sins secretly

11

Casting a Horoscope

The year, date, time of birth, latitude, and longitude of the place of birth are the essential data needed for casting a horoscope. Generally the time of birth of children born in India is recorded according to Indian Standard Time (IST), which has been chosen for maintaining uniformity throughout the country. The time of birth expressed in IST is first converted into Local Mean Time (LMT).

For calculations connected with the drawing up of a chart, one can conveniently use the two books — *Condensed Ephemeris of Planets' Positions* and *Tables of Ascendants* by Lahiri, prepared on the *Nirayana* (Indian) basis.

To illustrate the various steps in drawing up a chart, consider the example of a female born on October 1, 1968 at 3.25 a.m. at Neemuch, Madhya Pradesh.

Step 1. Find out the Local Mean Time (LMT) of birth.

The Local Mean Time (LMT) is required to determine the Sidereal Time[1] (ST) of a moment which is used in finding out the ascendant and the 10th house. The latitude and longitude of Neemuch are 24° - 27' North and 74° - 52' East, respectively. First of all, convert the IST 3.25 a.m. to LMT.

1. The distance measured along the celestial equator and expressed in hours.

		hrs.	min.	sec.
Local time correction for		3	25	0
Neemuch	-		30	32
Hence, LMT for Neemuch	=	2	54	28

Step 2. Find out the Sidereal Time (ST) of birth.

Sidereal Time (ST) for Oct. 1		12	38	8
Correction for 1968	+		2	5
Hence, ST for noon, Oct. 1, 1968	=	12	40	13
Correction for Neemuch	+			5
Hence, ST for noon, Oct. 1, 1968 at Neemuch	=	12	40	18

LMT is 2 hrs. 54 min. 28 sec. which is 9 hrs. 5 min. 32 sec. before noon of that date. This time interval increased by 10 sec. per hour becomes 9hrs. 7min. 2sec.

ST at Neemuch noon	=	12	40	18
Corrected time interval before noon (to be deducted from the ST at Neemuch noon)	-	9	7	2
Hence, ST of birth *(If LMT is after 12 noon, add the corrected time interval to the ST at noon).*	=	3	33	16

Step 3. Find out the longitude of the ascendant (Lagna).

As the latitude of Neemuch is		24°	-27'	N
Use the Table for the latitude		24°	-30'	N
For ST 3 hrs. 32 min. The Ascendant is		4^s	-3°	-38'
Proportional variation for 1 min. 16 secs.	+			13'
	=	4^s	- 3° -	51'
Hence, for ST 3 hrs. 33 min. 16 secs. the Ascendant is		4^s	- 3° -	51'
Ayanamsha correction for 1968	-			25'
	=	4^s	- 3°	- 26'

Hence the *Nirayana* ascendant is Leo with longitude 3° - 26'.

Note: This longitude is the middle point of the Ascendant.

Step 4. Find out the longitude of the 10th house.

For ST 3hrs. 32 min. the 10th house is		1^s - 2° - 21'
Here, variation for 4 min. is 58'		
Hence, Proportional variation for 1 min. = 15 sec.		1^s - 2° - 21'
	+	15'
		1^s - 2° - 36'
Ayanamsha correction	-	25'
	=	1^s - 2° - 11'

Therefore, the *Nirayana* 10th house falls in the sign Taurus with longitude 2° - 11'.

Step 5. Find out the longitudes of the remaining houses.

i.	Deduct the longitude of the 10th house from the longitude of the Ascendant (1st house)		4^s - 3° - 26'
		-	1^s - 2° - 11'
		=	3^s - 1° - 15'
ii.	Divide the above by 6 to get		15° - 12' - 30"
iii.	Multiply the above by 2 to get		1^s - 0° - 25'
iv.	Add the above to the longitude of the 10th house to find out		1^s - 2° - 11'
		+	1^s - 0° - 25'
	the longitude of the 11th house.	=	2^s - 2° - 36'
v.	Again add 1^s - 0° - 25' to the longitude of the 11th house to		2^s - 2° - 36'
		+	1^s - 0° - 25'
	find out the longitude of the 12th house.	=	3^s - 3° - 1'
vi.	Again add 1^s - 0° - 25' to the longitude of the 12th house to		3^s - 3° - 1'
		+	1^s - 0° - 25'
	find out the longitude of the Ascendant (1st House).	=	4^s - 3° - 26'

vii.	Add 2 signs to the longitude of the 12th house to get the longitude of the 2nd house.		3^s - 3° - 1'
			2^s - 0° - 0'
		=	5^s - 3° - 1'
viii.	Add 4 signs to the longitude of the 11th house to get the longitude of the 3rd house		2^s - 2° - 36'
		+	4^s - 0° - 0'
		=	6^s - 2° - 36'
ix.	Add 6 signs to the longitude of the 10th house to get the longitude of the 4th house		1^s - 2° - 11'
		+	6^s - 0° - 0'
		=	7^s - 2° - 11'
x.	Add 6 signs to the longitude of the 11th house to get the longitude of the 5th house		2^s - 2° - 36'
		+	6^s - 0° - 0'
		=	8^s - 2° - 36'
xi.	Add 6 signs to the longitude of the 12th house to get the longitude of the 6th house		3^s - 3° - 1'
		+	6^s - 0° - 0'
		=	9^s - 3° - 1'
xii.	Add 6 signs to the longitude of the 1st house to get the longitude of the 7th house		4^s - 3° - 26'
		+	6^s - 0° - 0'
		=	10^s - 3° - 26'
xiii.	Add 6 signs to the longitude of the 2nd house to get the longitude of the 8th house		5^s - 3° - 1'
		+	6^s - 0° - 0'
		=	11^s - 3° - 1'
xiv.	Add 6 signs to the longitude of the 3rd house to get the longitude of the 9th house		6^s - 2° - 36'
		+	6^s - 0° - 0'
		=	0^s - 2° - 36'

Note: Remember that all the above longitudes are the middle points of the various houses.

Step 6. Calculate the positions of planets.

The movement of the Moon from 5.30 a.m. of the given date up to the desired moment can be calculated according to its daily motion obtained from the Ephemeris.

The movement of the Sun and other planets from 5.30 a.m. of the preceeding date up to the desired moment can be calculated according to the motion for 4 days.

Following are the signs and longitudes of the various planets calculated for 3.25 a.m. on 1.10.1968.

Positions of Planets at 3.25 a.m. on Oct. 1, 1968.

Planets	*Longitude*
The Moon	$9^{s} - 6^{\circ} - 26'$
The Sun	$5^{s} - 14^{\circ} - 22'$
Mars	$4^{s} - 12^{\circ} - 18'$
Mercury	$6^{s} - 7^{\circ} - 8'$
Jupiter	$4^{s} - 27^{\circ} - 40'$
Venus	$6^{s} - 11^{\circ} - 45'$
Saturn	$11^{s} - 29^{\circ} - 47'$
Rahu	$11^{s} - 16^{\circ} - 8'$
Ketu	$5^{s} - 16^{\circ} - 8'$

Step 7. Draw a zodiacal diagram representing a picture of heavens at the time of birth of the girl.

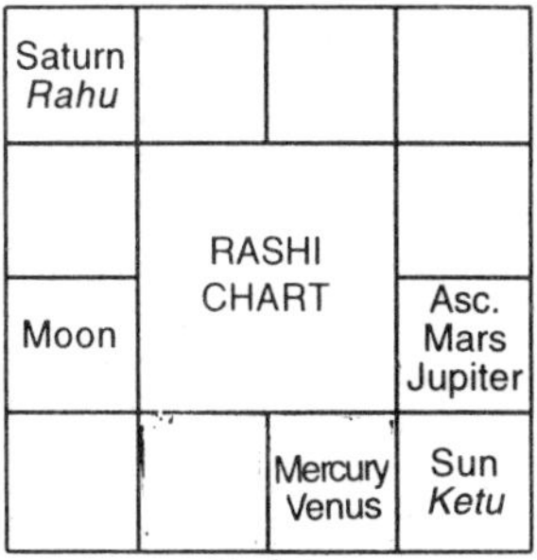

Fig. 33

Step 8. Find out the Nakshatras of the planets.

These can be found out from the Table given in Chapter 5.

Planet	*Longitude*	*Nakshatra*
The Sun	$5^{s} - 14^{\circ} - 22'$	*Hasta*
The Moon	$9^{s} - 6^{\circ} - 26'$	*U.Shadha*
Mars	$4^{s} - 12^{\circ} - 18'$	*Magha*
Mercury	$6^{s} - 7^{\circ} - 8'$	*Swati*
Jupiter	$4^{s} - 27^{\circ} - 40'$	*U.Phalguni*
Venus	$6^{s} - 11^{\circ} - 45'$	*Swati*
Saturn	$11^{s} - 29^{\circ} - 47'$	*Revati*
Rahu	$11^{s} - 16^{\circ} - 8'$	*U.Bhadra*
Ketu	$5^{s} - 16^{\circ} - 8'$	*Hasta*
Ascendant	$4^{s} - 3^{\circ} - 26'$	*Magha*

Step 9. Find out the Navamshas of different planets and the ascendant, and draw a Navamsha chart.*

The longitude of the ascendant is 3° - 26' in Leo. Consult the Table of *Navamshas* in Chapter 6. You will find that 3° - 26' falls in the 2nd *Navamsha*. This *Navamsha*, under the column of Leo, belongs to the sign Taurus. Thus, the *Lagna* of the *Navamsha* chart will be in the sign Taurus. Jupiter, for example, is in the sign Leo at a longitude of 27° - 40'. You will find under the column Leo that this longitude falls in the 9th *Navamsha* which is of the sign Sagittarius. The *Navamshas* of other planets may also be found out in the same way and a *Navamsha* chart may be drawn as shown below. Note that Saturn is in the *Vargottamamsha* as it occupies the same sign (that is, Pisces) both in the *Navamsha* and *Rashi* charts.

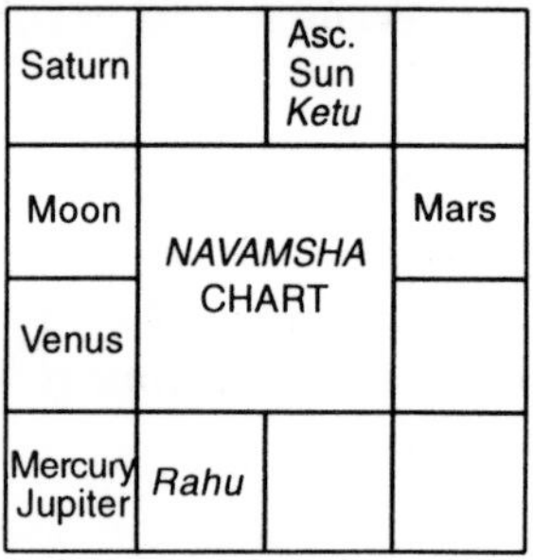

Fig. 34

Planet	*Longitude*	*Navamsha*
The Sun	$5^s - 14^\circ - 22'$	Taurus
The Moon	$9^s - 6^\circ - 26'$	Aquarius
Mars	$4^s - 12^\circ - 18'$	Cancer
Mercury	$6^s - 7^\circ - 8'$	Sagittarius
Jupiter	$4^s - 27^\circ - 40'$	Sagittarius
Venus	$6^s - 11^\circ - 45'$	Capricorn
Saturn	$11^s - 29^\circ - 47'$	Pisces
Rahu	$11^s - 16^\circ - 8'$	Scorpio
Ketu	$5^s - 16^\circ - 8'$	Taurus

* Steps 8 and 9 may be calculated after the horoscope has been drawn up.

PART TWO

Astrological Predictions

12

Predicting Educational Achievements

Certain houses and their significators, especially Mercury and Jupiter, are taken into consideration regarding the educational prospects of a native. Jupiter signifies knowledge and wisdom, and Mercury, intelligence. The 4th house in a horoscope signifies education; the 5th, intelligence and memory; the 2nd, speech; and the 9th, fortune or the native's chance of receiving education. All these are seldom found in a balanced manner in a horoscope. For example, a person may be educated, but may lack a good memory or fluency in speech.

Planets occupying the 4th house, those aspecting the 4th house, the lord of the 4th house, the *Navamsha* occupied by the lord of the 4th house, and the significators of the 4th house are all considered for predicting the educational level of the native.

It is not difficult to predict one's chance of acquiring education, but prediction regarding the type of education likely to be received by the native is a ticklish problem. The problem becomes all the more complex if we consider the large and diverse number of courses and subjects presently being taught at various levels. Moreover, our ancient astrological books dwell only on a limited number of branches of education. However, the planetary positions and strengths can certainly provide some clues regarding the native's inclination towards a particular subject. The Sun represents medicine; the Moon, nursing, agriculture, and marine engineering; Mars, military science, chemistry, medicine, and surgery; Mercury, literature, accountancy, astrology, mathematics, and printing technology; Jupiter, law, banking, and philosophy; Venus, music, fine arts, painting, and hotel management; Saturn, mining, metallurgy, leather technology, agriculture, engineering, and other scientific subjects.

Combinations for Higher Education: A person will receive a good education with the following combinations:

1. A strong and unafflicted Mercury.
2. The Lord of the 4th house is posited in the 4th house and aspected by, or conjoined with benefic planets.
3. Mercury or Venus is situated in the 4th house.
4. Jupiter is posited in a quadrant or a trine, and Venus is in her exaltation sign.
5. Both Venus and Jupiter are situated in a single house.
6. Mercury, Jupiter, and the lord of the 2nd house are posited in a quadrant or a trine, or in their own signs.
7. The Moon occupies Sagittarius which, in turn, is being aspected by benefic planets.
8. An exalted Jupiter occupies the 2nd house.
9. Mercury and Venus are posited in the 2nd or 3rd house.
10. Jupiter occupies the 2nd house from the Moon, while the lords of the 2nd and 4th houses are in the 9th house.
11. The ascendant is being occupied by the lords of the 2nd and 4th houses, and is aspected by Mercury.
12 Jupiter occupies the 2nd house and aspects the lord of the 2nd house.
13. Mars is at an angle to Mercury, while the Moon is at an angle to Venus.
14. The Moon is in the 9th house, and the 4th house is occupied by Mercury, along with the lords of the 1st and 9th houses.
15. Jupiter is placed in the 5th or 9th house from the

Moon, and Mars is in the 5th or 9th house from Mercury.

16. The lord of the 5th house occupies the 10th or 11th house.
17. Jupiter, which owns the 2nd house, is aspected by the Sun. (This is applicable only in Scorpio and Aquarius ascendants.)
18. Venus, which owns the 2nd house, is aspected by Mars. (This is applicable only in Aries and Virgo ascendants).
19. Mars occupies the 2nd house, and is aspected by a benefic planet.

Combinations for Ordinary Education: A person will receive only an ordinary education, or perhaps, no education with the following combinations:

1. The lord of the 4th house occupies the 6th, 8th, or 12th house.
2. The lord of the 4th house, together with Mercury and Jupiter, occupies the 6th, 9th, or 12th house.
3. The lord of the 5th house, together with Mercury and Jupiter, occupies the 6th, 8th, or 12th house.
4. The lord of the 2nd house, together with Mercury and Jupiter, occupies the 6th, 8th, or 12th house.
5. An afflicted and weak Mercury.

Examine Fig. 35 which is that of a university professor. Note that the significator of education (Mercury) is placed in its own sign, aspecting the 4th house, and is, in turn, aspected by Jupiter. Jupiter owns the 4th house, while the 1st and 10th houses are owned by Mercury. Saturn, lord of the 5th house, occupies its own sign. The 9th house is occupied by an exalted Moon, and the 2nd house by Jupiter.

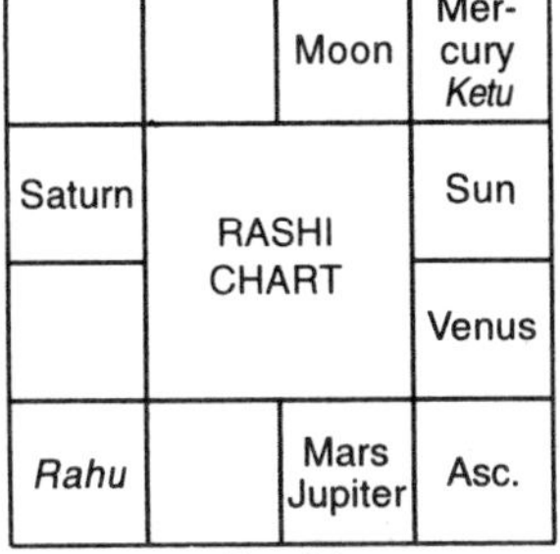

Fig. 35

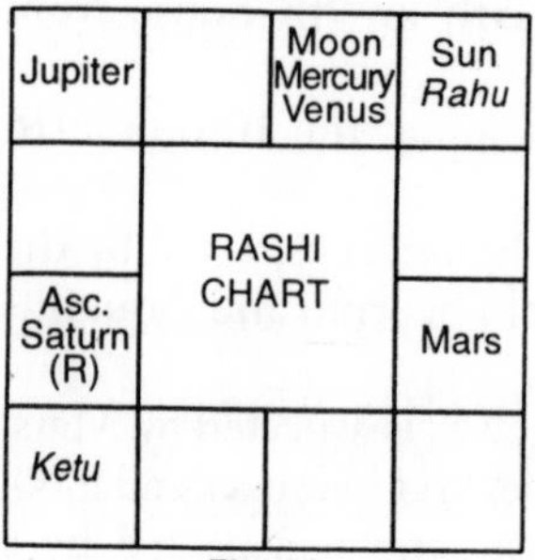

Fig. 36

Fig. 36 belongs to a native who received no education. Note that the lord of the 4th house (Mars) occupies the 8th house, and the lord of the 8th house, in turn, occupies the 6th house. The 4th house is afflicted by *Ketu's* aspect. Jupiter is aspected by Mars and Saturn. The 2nd and 4th houses counted from the Moon, are severely afflicted.

13

Predicting Favourable Careers and Professions

The 10th house in a horoscope signifies one's profession, status, authority, honour, and fame. The significators of the 10th house are the Sun, Mercury, Jupiter, and Saturn. In the present age it is often a very difficult decision to decide on one's means of livelihood on account of the variety of career options that are available. Lakhs of people pursue vocations quite contrary to their training, background, or potential. Planets occupying the 10th house or aspecting it, the lord of the 10th house, the *Navamsha* occupied by the lord of the 10th house, and the significators of the 10th house — all provide some definite guidelines for selecting one's profession.

The influence of a house cannot be judged in isolation. It is always interrelated with other houses. In the case of a career, the 10th house which determines the career is closely related to the 1st house which determines one's aptitude, the 2nd house which influences the native's income, the 9th house which dominates his fortune, and the 7th house which has a telling effect on partnerships.

Signs in the 10th House

The airy signs (Gemini, Libra, and Aquarius) indicate mental or intellectual pursuits, planning, oratory, and so on. The watery signs (Cancer, Scorpio, and Pisces) have a leaning towards occupations connected with liquids, travelling, dressmaking, hospitals, and navigation. The fiery signs (Aries, Leo, and Sagittarius) are inclined towards professions linked with fire, iron, metals, surgery, and factories. The earthy signs (Taurus, Virgo, and Capricorn) are favourable for business and indicate professions which involve patience, practical ability, and labour.

Planets in the 10th House

Different planets in the 10th house motivate the native towards a particular profession, job, or vocation.

Generally speaking, Mercury and Jupiter refer to intellectual professions, trade, and business; Venus, to aesthetic professions; the Sun, the Moon, and Mars, to economic activity; Saturn, to jobs requiring a mechanical mind and hard work; *Rahu* and *Ketu* to routine jobs.

Jupiter is prominent in the charts of lawyers, whereas Mars and the Sun dominate the charts of engineers. The Sun, Mars, and Jupiter are prominent in the charts of doctors. Artists and musicians have a strong Moon and Venus, coupled with benefic aspects from Mercury, Mars, and the Sun. Journalists and editors have a strong Moon, Mercury, and Jupiter. Accountants have a strong Moon and Mercury. Teachers and professors have a strong Mercury and Jupiter. Astrologers have a strong Moon, Mercury, and Saturn.

Planets	*Suitable Professions*
The Sun	Ministers, govt. officials, magistrates, doctors
The Moon	Travellers, sailors, fishermen, nurses
Mars	Surgeons, chemists, butchers, police and military personnel, metallurgists, lawyers, realtors, machinists
Mercury	Poets, authors, editors, printers, accountants, teachers, astrologers, mathematicians
Jupiter	Teachers, judges, physicians, lawyers, priests, bankers, philosophers
Venus	Artists, actors, musicians, jewellers, perfume sellers
Saturn	Agriculturists, gardeners, philosophers, masons, miners, scavengers

Combinations for Professional Status and Fame

1. If the 10th house and its lord are related by conjunction or aspect with benefic planets, the native will earn both respect and position in his profession.
2. If the lords of the 9th and the 10th houses exchange places, that is, the lord of the 9th house is in the 10th house and vice versa, the native will enjoy much fame and honour.
3. The presence of Mars or the Sun in the 10th house elevates a person to a higher position, thus giving him greater authority.
4. The native will be a high-ranking person if the lords of the 5th and 10th houses are posited in their respective houses.
5. If the lord of the 1st house occupies the 9th house, and the lord of the 10th occupies the 1st, the native will be a famous man with a high status.

The native will be unfortunate in respect of the 10th house matters if a debilitated planet is posited in the 10th house.

If the lord of the 10th house occupies the 6th, 8th, or 12th house, the person concerned will not achieve a high position in his career, and will also be troubled by enemies or diseases.

The *Rashi* chart in Fig. 37 is that of a government official. Note the fine position of Venus (the *Yogakaraka* planet when Aquarius is the ascendant) in the house of profession with the significator of profession, Mercury. Mars, the lord of the 10th house, is aspected by the significators Jupiter and Saturn. However, Jupiter as lord of the 2nd house, has a negative influence on Mars and has curtailed the longevity of the native. The native started his career from a low position, rose to a high status, and attained financial prosperity.

The *Rashi* chart in Fig. 38 is that of a rich and professionally successful medical doctor. The 10th house prospects are quite bright as all the significators of profession — the Sun, Mercury, Jupiter, and Saturn — are in mutual aspect. The Sun, which indicates the medical profession, is

Saturn	*Ketu*		
Asc. Moon	RASHI	CHART	
Jupiter			
	Mercury Venus	Sun *Rahu*	Mars

Fig. 37

Mars		Asc. Jupiter Saturn	Moon
Ketu	RASHI	CHART	
Venus			*Rahu*
	Sun Mercury		

Fig. 38

aspecting Saturn, the lord of the 10th house. Counted from the Moon, Mars occupies the 10th house, again indicating the medical profession. Mark the position of the lords of the 4th and 5th houses in the 7th house, and the exchange between the lords of the 1st and 9th houses. The mutual aspect between Mercury, lord of the 2nd house, and Jupiter, lord of the 11th house, indicates a sound financial position.

The *Rashi* chart in Fig. 39 is that of a chemical engineer, serving in the Indian Oil Corporation. Note that the Moon is exalted in the 9th house, and the lord of the 9th house, Venus, is conjoined with the lord of the 1st and 10th houses (Mercury). Saturn and Jupiter, occupy their own signs. Note the fine aspects of Saturn on Jupiter, Jupiter on *Lagna,* and Mercury and Venus on the 10th house.

Jupiter		Moon	*Rahu*
	RASHI CHART		
Saturn			Uranus
Mars Mercury Venus, *Ketu*	Sun	Neptune	Asc.

Fig. 39

The *Rashi* chart in Fig. 40 belongs to a bank officer. Here the significator and lord of the 10th house, Jupiter, is aspecting the 10th house. Saturn, the lord of the 9th house, is aspecting Mercury, which indicates work connected with finance and accounts. Counted from the Moon, the 10th house has Saturn, while the lord of the 10th house, Mars, is associated with Mercury. The chart indicates a steady flow of income as the Moon, the lord of the 2nd house, and Mars, the lord of the 11th house, are in mutual aspect.

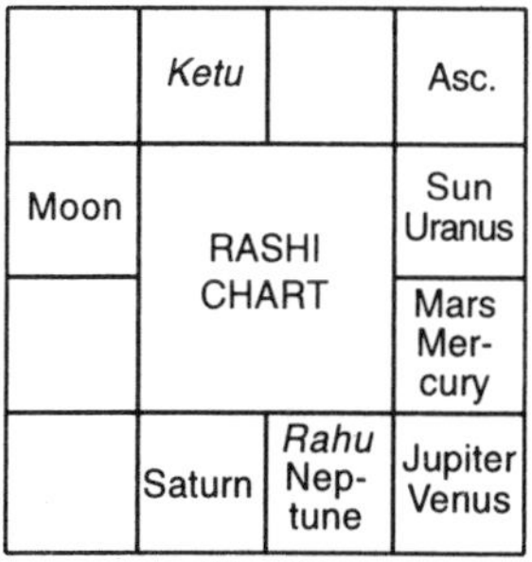

Fig. 40

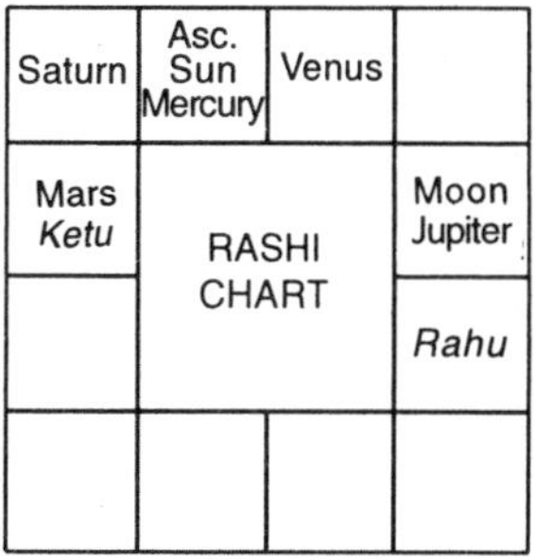

Fig. 41

The *Rashi* chart in Fig. 41 belongs to a successful lawyer. Note the auspicious combination of the Moon, the lord of the 4th house, and Jupiter, the lord of the 9th house, in the sign Cancer. Jupiter, signifying legal affairs, is aspecting the 10th house and its lord, Saturn. Counted from the Moon, the 10th house is tenanted by the Sun and Mercury — both significators of profession. The lords of the ascendant and 11th house are aspecting the lord of the 2nd house, Venus, indicating an excellent income. The lord of the ascendant is in a favourable house.

14

Predicting Wealth, Success and Prosperity

It is proverbially said that money makes the mare go. True, money is powerful and gives us much of what we desire in this world. It provides us with good food, beautiful clothes, and luxuries. A rich man commands respect and is considered a successful man. Though saints may decry the earning and accumulation of wealth as an undesirable practice, the fact is that we all aspire to become rich. Certainly wealth is a great force and we all want to acquire it.

Wealth has got to be earned and there are many ways to do so, all of them not always fair. Some acquire wealth by honest means, and others, by hook or crook. Some earn it by dint of hard work; others simply inherit it from their parents, in-laws, or other relatives. Still others become suddenly wealthy on account of receiving huge sums of money through lotteries, horse-racing, smuggling, and so on.

Though the 2nd house in a horoscope rules over wealth, certain other houses also have a say in this matter. The 9th house is an important trine and is called the House of Fortune. The 10th house indicates the type of occupation or means of livelihood. The 1st, 5th, and 9th houses are positioned 5th from one another, and act as a sort of a tripod on which the strength of a natal chart depends. The 11th is the house of gains. It is 180° from the 5th house. Therefore, the benefic planets in the 5th house may favourably aspect the 11th house and thus add to the vitality of the latter. The 8th house indicates unearned wealth or a legacy. The 8th house is in opposition to the 2nd house. Any beneficial planet in the 8th, especially Mercury, confers prosperity on the native. The significator of wealth and various type of gains is Jupiter. Obviously Jupiter should be strong in respect of a house or sign to be able to provide a good income. With this overview, let us now look at some indications of acquiring wealth.

Combinations for Acquiring Wealth: Planets occupying the 2nd house or aspecting it, the lord of the 2nd house, the *Navamsha* occupied by the lord of the 2nd, and the significator of the 2nd house (Jupiter) are the main considerations in this connection. A person will have a lot of wealth if:

1. The 1st, 2nd, and 11th houses are occupied respectively by their lords.
2. The lord of the 2nd or 11th house is posited in the 11th house either in a friendly sign or exalted sign, or in its own sign.
3. The lords of the 2nd and 11th houses are mutual friends and occupy the ascendant.
4. The lords of the 1st, 2nd, and 11th houses occupy the ascendant.
5. The Moon occupies the 2nd house and is aspected by Venus.
6. Mercury occupies the 2nd house, and is aspected by a benefic planet.
7. The lords of the 2nd and 11th houses occupy a quadrant, that is, the 1st, 4th, 7th, or the 10th houses.
8. The lord of the 2nd house is in the 11th house, and the lord of the 11th house is in the 2nd or 11th house.
9. The benefic planets occupy the *Upachaya* houses (3rd, 6th, 10th, and 11th), counted either from the *Lagna* or the Moon; this is the famous *Vasumati Yoga*.
10. The lord of the 2nd house is exalted and is aspected by Jupiter.

11. The lord of the 2nd house occupies the 9th, 10th, or the 11th house.
12. The lords of the 2nd and 10th houses are conjoined in a quadrant or a trine.
13. The lord of the ascendant is posited in the 9th or the 2nd house.
14. The lord of the 11th house is placed in the ascendant; the lord of the ascendant in the 2nd house; and the lord of the 2nd in the 11th house.
15. Venus and the Moon occupy the 12th house.
16. The benefic planets occupy the 8th house.
17. The lord of the 12th house is in an exalted position and aspected by the lord of the 9th house.
18. Mercury and Venus occupy the 2nd house.

The horoscope of an industrialist, Mr Ramkrishna Dalmia, given in Fig. 42 is an illustration of a very wealthy man. The 2nd house in a horoscope rules over wealth. Note that the lord of the 2nd house, the Moon, is posited in the 7th house, from where it is aspecting the *Lagna*. Both the significator of wealth — Jupiter, and the lord of the 11th house — Mars, are aspecting the Moon.

Jupiter and *Rahu* are powerful in the 11th house. All the trines are interrelated as the lords of the 1st (Mercury), 5th (Venus), and 9th (Saturn) are in mutual aspect. The 12th lord, Venus, is exalted and is in aspect to the 9th lord, Saturn. Besides, there is *Malavya Yoga* (see Chapter 22).

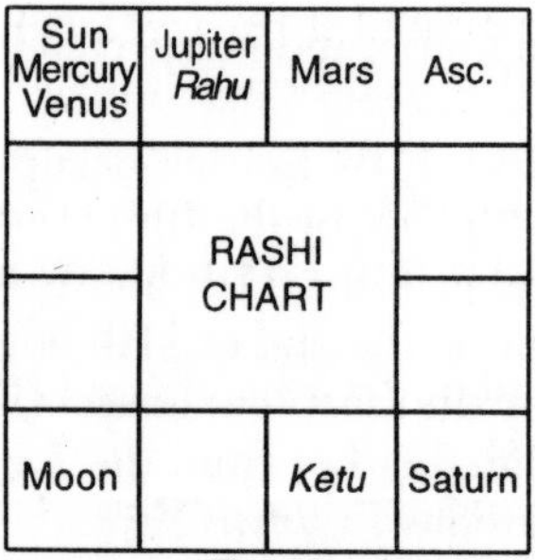

Fig. 42

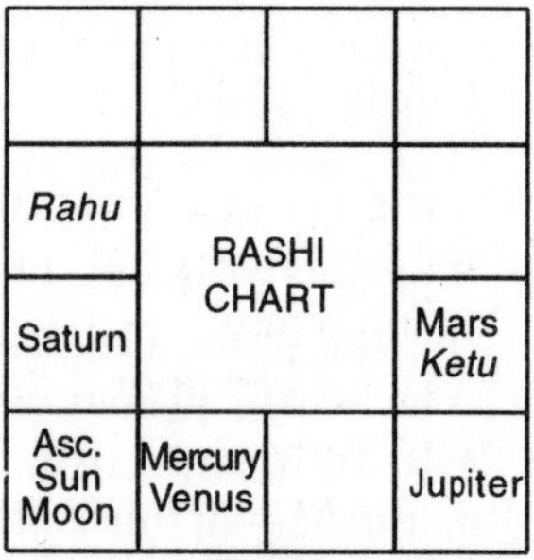

Fig. 43

Another notable chart (Fig. 43) is that of Mr Dhirubhai

Ambani, a famous businessman and industrialist. Saturn, the lord of the 2nd house is posited in the 2nd house. Jupiter, as lord of the ascendant as well as significator of wealth, is aspecting the 2nd house and its lord, Saturn. Jupiter is also posited in an angle from the Moon, causing the *Gajakeshari Yoga*. *Rahu* is favourable in the 3rd house. The lord of the 9th house, the Sun, is in the *Lagna*, and the lord of the 5th house, Mars, is in the 9th house. The position of Venus in the 12th house is fine regarding acquisition of money.

Combinations for Poverty/Loss of Money: A person of ordinary means, leading a hand-to-mouth existence, is considered poor. The causes of poverty may be many. For example, a person may not have received a good education/ training, or have found a suitable job. He may have inherited debts, or may be mentally or physically sick. These are some of the causes which may affect his financial status.

There are certain bad combinations, as detailed below, which can indicate poverty:

1. If the lord of the 2nd house is in the 6th or 12th house, there will be loss of wealth.
2. There will be loss of money if the lord of the 12th house is in the 2nd house, and the lord of the 11th house occupies the 6th, 8th, or 12th house.
3. The native will be poor if the *Lagna* lord is in the 12th house, and the 12th lord is in the *Lagna*.
4. A weak financial status is indicated if the lord of the 2nd house is debilitated and placed between malefic planets.
5. Poverty is indicated if the lord of the 2nd house is in the 12th house, and the lord of the 12th house is in the 2nd house.
6. A man will be poor if the lord of the 6th, 8th, or 12th house occupies the 2nd house.
7. If the 2nd house, its lord, and the lord of the 11th house are all conjoined with malefics, the native will be poor.

8. If a malefic planet occupies the 2nd, 4th, or 5th house calculated from Jupiter (significator of wealth), the person will be poor.
9. When the Moon and the Sun in the ascendant are conjoined with, or aspected by the lord of the 2nd or the 7th house, the native remains a poor man.
10. The bad *Yogas* like *Daridra, Shakata,* and *Kemadruma* make a person poor and unlucky.

The chart of a person who cannot be considered fortunate as far as a steady income and permanent service are concerned is shown in Fig. 44.

Mars	Asc. Jupiter	Sun Venus *Rahu*	Mercury
	RASHI CHART		
	Saturn *Ketu*		Moon

Fig. 44

It may be noted that Venus, (the lord of the 2nd house, both from the *Lagna* and the Moon), indicating finance, is combust. The lord of the 10th and 11th houses, Saturn, is in the 8th house, and Mars as the *Lagna* lord is in the 12th house. The lords of the 9th (Jupiter) and 10th houses (Saturn) are at a six-eighth angle from each other. The 2nd house, its lord, and the lord of the 11th house are all conjoined with evil planets. The lord of the *Lagna* is in the 12th house, and the lord of the 12th is in the *Lagna*. There are also inauspicious *Yogas* like *Shakata* and *Kemadruma*. All these combinations do not bode well for the financial and career prospects of the native.

15

Predicting Love, Romance & Marriage

The 7th house should be studied for marriage prospects, nature of the partner, and married life. In a male chart the 7th house signifies the wife, and in a female chart, the husband. Planets occupying or aspecting the 7th house, the lord of the 7th house, the *Navamsha* occupied by the lord of the 7th house, and the significator of the 7th house (Venus) — should all be examined for predicting marriage and marital happiness.

Though the general rules regarding the 7th house are the same for men and women, there are some special points which need consideration in the female charts. The marital life or *Mangalya* of a female is judged from her 8th house; her children are examined from the 5th and the 9th; her beauty, appearance, and complexion can be seen from the ascendant; her general happiness, husband's character, and sexual passions from the 7th house; and chastity from the 4th. If the *Lagna* and the Moon fall in even signs, the girl will be endowed with feminine characteristics and will be beautiful. If the *Lagna* and the Moon fall in odd signs, she will be masculine in temperament and character. If one of the above falls in an odd sign and the other in an even sign, the female will have mixed characteristics.

Characteristics of Females Born in Different Ascendants

Ascendants	*Characteristics*
Aries	Truthful, quarrelsome, cruel
Taurus	Polite, agreeable, obedient
Gemini	Ill-tempered, sensuous
Cancer	Wealthy, polite, attractive, happy
Leo	Charitable, quarrelsome
Virgo	Good-tempered, doer of good deeds, happy
Libra	Lazy, sinful,proud
Scorpio	Virtuous, truthful
Sagittarius	Unkind, cruel
Capricorn	Good-charactered, well spoken of
Aquarius	Virtuous, grateful
Pisces	Beautiful, kind-hearted

Characteristics of Females Born in Different Moon Signs

Moon Signs	*Characteristics*
Aries	Fond of husband and work, devoted to elders
Taurus	Devoted to husband, wealthy, good-tempered
Gemini	Good-charactered, pleasant appearance, helpful to others
Cancer	Sickly, religious-minded, dignified
Leo	Beautiful, even-tempered, happy
Virgo	Virtuous, wealthy
Libra	Virtuous, sympathetic, possessing little sexual passion
Scorpio	Wealthy, unsympathetic
Sagittarius	Polite, charitable, sympathetic
Capricorn	Truthful, good-tempered
Aquarius	Virtuous, wealthy, charitable
Pisces	Modest, good-charactered, pleasant features, charitable

Characteristics of Females Born Under Different *Janma Nakshatras*

Janma Nakshatras	*Characteristics*
Ashwini	Bright and small eyes, sweet speech, ordinary married life
Bharani	Beautiful, bold, good character, good married life
Krittika	Good-looking, quarrelsome, unhappy married life
Rohini	Beautiful, possessing attractive eyes, short-tempered, good married life
Mrigashirsha	Lean, beautiful, greedy, good marriage
Ardra	Beautiful eyes, fault-finder, unhappy married life
Punarvasu	Curly hair, red eyes, sweet speech, happy married life
Pushya	Short, sincere, satisfactory married life
Ashlesha	Pleasant-looking, careless, satisfactory married life
Magha	Beautiful, helpful, short-tempered, satisfactory married life
Poorvaphalguni	Round face, polite, charitable, happy married life
Uttaraphalguni	Cool temperament, happy married life
Hasta	Attractive, happy married life
Chitra	Beautiful, sinful, unhappy married life
Swati	Truthful, virtuous, satisfactory married life
Vishakha	Beautiful, sweet-tongued, happy married life
Anuradha	Beautiful, pleasant, happy marriage
Jyeshtha	Broad face, emotional, ordinary married life
Moola	Obstinate, pure-hearted, satisfactory married life
Poorvashadha	Beautiful, possessing attractive eyes, straightforward, happy married life
Uttarashadha	Obstinate, religious, attractive eyes, prominent nose, satisfactory married life

Janma Nakshatras	Characteristics
Shravana	Tall body, prominent nose, talkative, religious, satisfactory married life
Dhanishtha	Attractive, extravagant, satisfactory married life
Shatabhishaka	Tall,short-tempered, God-fearing, unhappy married life
Poorvabhadrapada	Beautiful, sincere, possessing an optimistic outlook, happy married life
Uttarabhadrapada	Big eyes, cordial nature, happy married life
Revati	Beautiful, religious, stubborn, happy married life

Nature of Husband

If the 7th house is neither occupied nor aspected by benefic planets, the girl's husband will be an ordinary man. If the Sun is posited in the 7th house, the husband will live away from her. The husband will be poor and lustful if the 7th house is occupied by Mars; happy and learned, if occupied by Mercury; gentle and moral, if occupied by Jupiter; ease-loving and handsome, if occupied by Venus; ugly-looking and foolish, if occupied by Saturn.

Combinations for a Virtuous Wife and Happy Married Life: The native's wife will live long and be good-natured if the lord of the 7th house, counted either from the ascendant or the Moon, is associated with, or aspected by a benefic planet. Similar will be the case if the 7th house itself is occupied or aspected by its own lord, or by the lord of the 9th house. For a happy married life it is essential that the significator of the 7th house, Venus, is posited in a friendly sign, or conjoined with, or aspected by a benefic planet.

1. If the lord of the 7th house or Venus is conjoined with, or aspected by a benefic planet, or is situated between benefic planets, the wife of the person concerned will be beautiful and good-natured.

2. If the lord of the 7th house is conjoined with the lord of the ascendant, the native's married life will be happy.
3. If the 7th house, its lord, and Venus are all present in even signs, the wife will be beautiful and virtuous.
4. If the Moon occupies the 1st or the 7th house in her own or exaltation sign, and is aspected by a benefic planet, the wife will be virtuous.
5. When benefic planets occupy the 2nd, 7th, and 11th houses counted from the lord of the 7th house, the native's married life will be a happy one.
6. When the lords of the *Lagna* and the 7th house are friends, and not afflicted in any way, the relationship between the partners will be a happy one.

Combinations Resulting in an Unhappy Married Life: The native's conjugal life will not be happy if there are malefics in the 4th, 8th, or the 12th house from Venus; or if Venus is surrounded by, or conjoined with, or aspected by malefic planets. Similarly, if the 7th house or its lord is afflicted, the native's married life will not be happy.

1. If the Sun is in the ascendant, and Saturn is in the 7th house, the native may lose his wife.
2. If Saturn is in the 8th house, Mars in the 6th, and *Rahu* in the 7th, the native may lose his wife.
3. If the Moon occupies the 7th house and is aspected by malefics, the female concerned may become a widow at an early age.
4. A debilitated Jupiter in the 7th house, or Venus in the sign Scorpio in the 7th house, indicates loss of the native's wife.
5. If Taurus is the 7th house and is occupied by Mercury, there will be danger to the wife of the native.
6. If Venus is situated between two malefics, or if malefics are situated in the 2nd, 4th, or the 8th house from Venus, the native's married life will not be happy.
7. If *Rahu*, together with Saturn and Mars, joins the 7th

or the 8th house, early widowhood is indicated.

8. When the lord of the 7th house is retrograde, the native's married life will remain unhappy.

Combinations for a Love Marriage: While marriage prospects are indicated by the 7th house and its lord, a love affair leading to a successful marriage is judged from the 5th house and its lord. Besides, the manner in which Venus, the significator of marriage, aspects the Sun and the Moon, is also important in predicting the possibility of a love marriage. Some combinations which make for a love marriage are as follows:

1. The lord of the 5th house has some relation with Venus or the lord of the 7th house.
2. Venus has some relation with the lord of the 7th house.
3. The lord of the *lagna* has some relation with the lords of the 5th and 7th houses.
4. The lords of the 7th and 9th houses are posited in the 7th house.
5. The Moon and Venus are conjoined in the 7th house.
6. The Sun and Jupiter are conjoined in the 5th house.
7. An unafflicted Venus occupies the 5th house.

The prospects of a love marriage are best illustrated in Fig. 40 in Chapter 13. Note the auspicious position of the lord of the 7th house (Jupiter) with the lord of the 5th (Venus) in the 4th house. This native got married to a girl with whom he was in love for several years.

Combinations for a Delayed Marriage/Unmarried State: The marriage of a boy/girl is likely to be delayed or not take place at all if one or more of the following combinations are present in the birth chart:

1. Saturn occupies the 7th house from the *Lagna* or the Moon, and is aspected by a malefic planet.
2. The lord of the 7th house is associated with, or is in opposition to Saturn.
3. Venus is in conjunction with, or in opposition to Saturn.

4. The lord of the 7th house is posited in an evil house, that is, the 12th, 8th, or 6th house counted from the 7th house.
5. Mars and the Sun, or Mars and the Moon are posited in the 7th house.
6. *Rahu* combines with Venus in the *Lagna* or in the 7th house.
7. The 7th house is owned by a malefic planet, and other malefics join or aspect the same.
8. The 7th house is owned by a malefic planet, and the Moon and a malefic planet are also posited in it.
9. Mercury and Venus conjoin in the 7th house, and are afflicted by evil planets.
10. *Rahu* is in the 7th house, and is either aspected by or conjoined with malefic planets.
11. The lord of the 7th house is malefic, and the significator, Venus, is weak.
12. The Sun, Mars, Venus, and Jupiter are posited in the 10th house.
13. The lords of the 2nd and 7th houses are conjoined with a malefic, and Venus is in an evil house.

The *Rashi* chart in Fig.45 is that of an unmarried lady. Note that the significator of marriage, Venus, and the lord of the 7th house, the Moon, are in the 12th house, and are

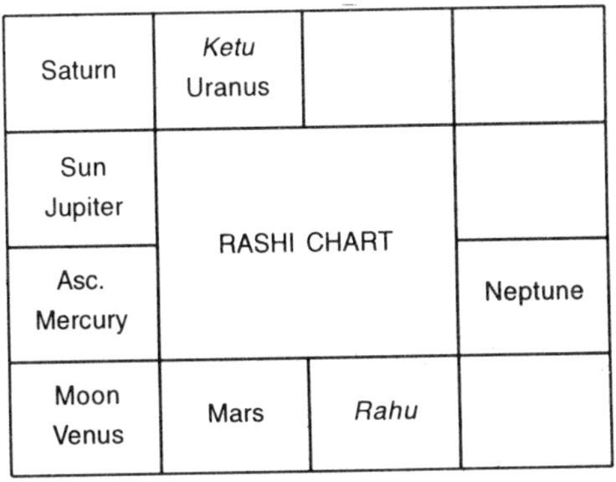

Fig. 45

aspected by Saturn. The 2nd house, signifying family, is occupied by the evil planets — the Sun, and Jupiter (lords of the 8th and 12th houses, respectively), which are further aspected by Mars and *Rahu*. The 4th house, indicating happiness, is tenanted by two malefics, Uranus and *Ketu*.

Combinations Leading to Separation/Divorce: Discord in marital life can be attributed to three factors: emotional instability or immaturity of the married partners; an unsatisfactory sex life; and outside influences, such as social, economic, and parental.

Astrology enables us to read the indications and tendencies for a happy or unhappy married life. Certain combinations that forebode the separation of married couples are given below:

1. The lord of the 7th house occupies the 6th house, and is afflicted.
2. Venus or the lord of the 7th house joins with the lord of the 6th house, and they are also associated with or aspected by malefic planets.
3. *Rahu* and Saturn are present in the ascendant.
4. Jupiter occupies Libra and is posited in the 7th house.
5. The lords of the 1st and 7th houses are placed in a six-eighth or two-twelfth position from each other.
6. The Sun and Mars occupy the 2nd, 7th, or 8th house.

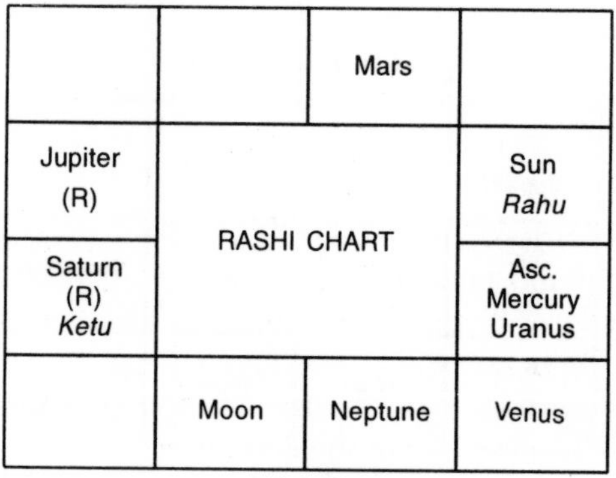

Fig. 46

7. The 7th house is occupied by the Sun in a female's horoscope.

Now let us examine Fig.46 of a lady separated from her husband. Note that the 7th house is occupied by retrograde Jupiter. Saturn, the lord of the 7th house, is also retrograde and is aspected by *Rahu.* The significator, Venus, is debilitated and sandwiched by malefics. The ascendant lord, the Sun, is in the 12th house with *Rahu.* The ascendant is joined with the evil Mercury.

Combinations for Promiscuous Relationships: Venus and the 7th house rule over the sex life of the husband, while the 7th house and Mars govern the sex life of the wife. The 6th and 12th houses dominate extramarital relationships in both cases. Some combinations resulting in extramarital relationships or a promiscuous sex life are given below:

1. Two or more malefic planets are present in the 7th house.
2. The 7th house is aspected by a strong Venus.
3. An afflicted Venus is in the 7th house, and is not aspected by or conjoined with any benefic planet.
4. Venus is in the 10th house from the Moon, and Saturn is in the 10th house from Venus.
5. The lord of the 7th house is conjoined with *Rahu* or *Ketu,* and is aspected by or conjoined with a malefic planet.
6. Mercury is in the 7th house in the sign Pisces, or is in an inimical sign.
7. The lord of the 7th house along with Venus occupy an evil house.
8. The lords of the 2nd, 6th, and 7th houses, along with Venus and a malefic planet, occupy the *Lagna.*
9. The lords of the *Lagna,* 2nd and 6th houses, are in the 7th house, and in association with a malefic planet.
10. The lords of the 6th and 7th houses, along with a malefic planet are in the 2nd house.
11. Saturn, Mars, and the Moon occupy the 7th house.

12. A waning Moon is in the 7th house in Scorpio or in an inimical sign.
13. The lord of the 8th house, being a malefic, is posited in the 8th house, and is conjoined with or aspected by other malefic planets.
14. The 7th house is owned by Mars or Saturn, and either of them, along with the Moon and Saturn, are present there.
15. The lord of the 7th house is in the 6th, 8th, or 12th house, and is conjoined with or aspected by Mars and Saturn.
16. Venus occupies either the 6th, 8th, or 12th house, and is afflicted by a malefic planet.

Now re-examine Fig.46. Note that the lord of the 7th house, Saturn, is in the 6th house with *Ketu.* The 2nd and 4th houses are occupied by a debilitated Venus and the Moon, respectively. Counted from the Moon, Mars is posited in the 7th house, the lord of which is in debilitation. The ascendant is occupied by a combust Mercury. This combination shows that the lady is leading a questionable moral life.

Matching of Horoscopes

A very important consideration at the time of matching horoscopes for marriage is the deposition of Mars in certain houses. The presence of Mars in certain houses is deemed to be a defect. A person is said to be *Mangalika* when Mars is deposited in the 2nd, 4th, 7th, 8th, or 12th house (some astrologers include the 1st house too) from the *Lagna*, the Moon, or Venus. A marriage between a boy having this *Mangalika* defect and a girl not having it is treated as incompatible. However, if Mars is posited in any one of the above houses in a girl's horoscope, the defect is deemed to be nullified. The same is true if *Rahu*, the Sun, or Saturn is posited in any one of the above houses. The *Mangalika* defect is deemed to be nullified if Jupiter is placed in a trine or an angle; or if Mars is in Aries in the 1st house, in Scorpio in the 4th house, in Pisces in the 7th house, in Aquarius in the

8th house, or in Sagittarius in the 12th house. In such cases, the marriage between the two will not be harmful.

There are many complicated rules for matching horoscopes. The following guidelines should, however, be sufficient for the purpose of this elementary book.

1. If the *Janma Rashi* of the boy is 7th, 10th, or 11th when counted from the *Janma Rashi* of the girl, it makes for a favourable marriage.
2. If in the horoscopes of the boy and girl in question, the lords of the ascendant and lords of the *Janma Rashi* are friendly, the marriage prospects will be good.
3. If the *Nakshatra* of the boy is 4th, 7th, 10th, 13th, 16th, 19th, 22nd, or 25th when counted from the *Nakshatra* of the girl, it is auspicious for the marriage.
4. Count the number of *Nakshatras* from *Ashwini* to that of the *Nakshatra* of the boy. Similarly, count the number of *Nakshatras* from *Ashwini* to that of the girl's. Add both the numbers, and then add 13 to the total. Subtract 32 from the total sum and divide by 5. If the remainder is 0, 1, or 3, it is good for the marriage.
5. Count the number of *Nakshatras* from that of the boy up to *Ashwini*. Do the same count for the girl.Add the two figures and divide by 5. If the remainder is 1,2, or 4, a happy and prosperous married life is assured.

Timing of the Marriage

It would be considered auspicious to fix the marriage of the native when any one of the following conditions is satisfied:

1. The lord of the ascendant transits the 7th house.
2. Jupiter transits the house occupied by Venus or by the lord of the 7th house.
3. Venus or the lord of the 7th house transits the sign occupied by the lord of the ascendant, or a sign which is at the 5th or 9th position from it.
4. Venus or the lord of the 7th house transits the *Navamsha* occupied by the lord of the ascendant, or a sign which is at the 5th or 9th position from it.

16

Predicting the Birth of Children

The 5th house in a horoscope indicates children. The significator of this house is Jupiter. Though this house is mainly examined for predicting the birth of children, we must examine other houses as well, such as the 1st and the 9th, which also play an important role in this connection. The ascendant indicates everything that affects the native. The 9th house indicates one's fortune. A man is considered unlucky if he has no child. Therefore these houses as well as the significator, Jupiter, should be strong if the native is destined to have children and derive happiness through them.

Combinations for Birth of Children: Planets occupying the 5th house, those aspecting the 5th house, the lord of the 5th house, the *Navamsha* occupied by the lord of the 5th, and the significator of the 5th house, Jupiter, are important in this connection. Several possible combinations are given below:

1. Jupiter and the lords of the 5th house, both counted from the ascendant and the Moon, are well placed.
2. The 5th house is conjoined with or aspected by benefic planets.
3. The lords of the ascendant and the 5th house are posited together, or aspect each other, or are in each other's houses.

4. The lord of the 5th house is associated with or aspected by a benefic planet, or occupies the ascendant or the 5th house.
5. The lord of the ascendant is in the 5th house, and the lord of the 5th house and Jupiter are strong.
6. The lords of the 5th and 9th houses join in a friendly sign in aspect to a benefic planet.
7. Jupiter is in the 5th house, and the lord of the 5th house is strong, and in aspect to a benefic planet.
8. Jupiter is in the 5th house, in aspect to the lord of the 5th house.
9. The first child will be a male if the lord of the 1st house is in the 2nd, 3rd, or 1st house.
10. The first child will be a female if the lord of the 1st house is in the 4th house.
11. There will be several sons if the lords of the 5th house, the Sun, Mars, and Jupiter are posited in male signs or *Navamshas*.
12. There will be many sons if the 5th house or its lord is situated in a male sign or *Navamsha,* or is in conjunction with, or aspected by male planets.
13. There will be female progeny if the 5th house or its lord is situated in a female sign or *Navamsha,* or is in conjunction with, or aspected by female planets.
14. There will be female children if the lord of the 5th or 9th house occupies the 7th house or a female sign, and is conjoined with, or aspected by the Moon or Venus.

The *Rashi* chart in Fig. 47 belongs to a native with many children, mostly sons. Observe that the 5th house is in a male sign with the lord of the ascendant, Mars (a male planet), posited therein. Counted from the Moon, the 5th and 9th houses are male signs. The significator, Jupiter, occupying a male sign, is aspecting the 9th and 11th houses. From the Moon, Jupiter is posited in the 9th house itself. The dispositor of Jupiter, Mercury, is with the lord of the 5th house.

In Fig. 48 note that the 1st, 5th, and 9th houses fall in

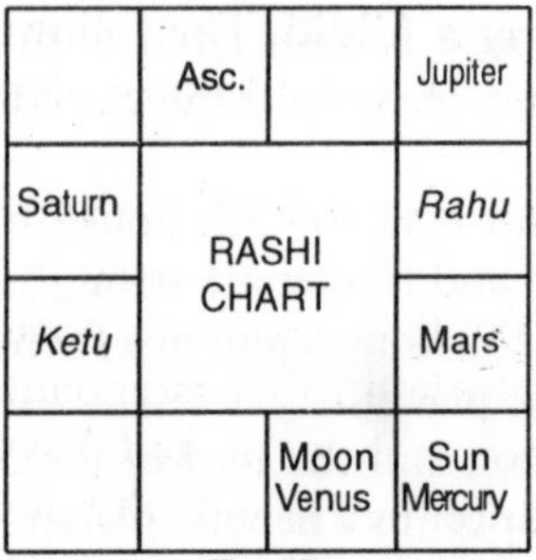

Fig. 47

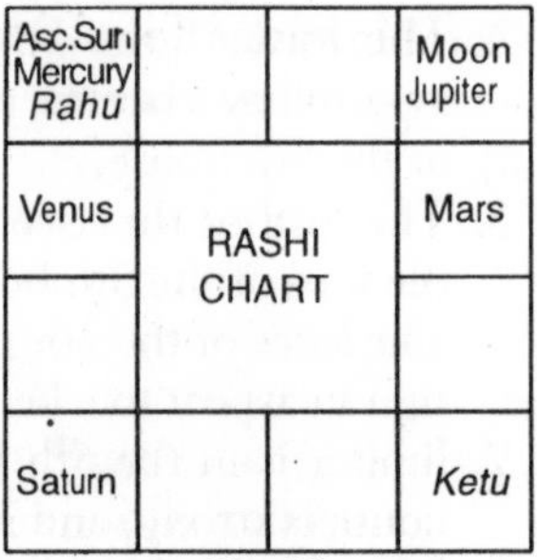

Fig. 48

the female signs. The lords of the 1st (Jupiter) and 5th house (the Moon) are aspected by the malefic Saturn. The 5th house is tenanted by a debilitated Mars. The dispositor of the Moon and Jupiter — Mercury — is debilitated and with malefics. Counted from the Moon, the 5th house lord, Venus, is a female planet and, in turn, aspected by Saturn. The native of this chart was blessed with three daughters and no son.

Combinations for a Few Children: The following combinations indicate the birth of a few children after much delay:

1. An *Alpasuta* sign is in the 5th house — the signs Taurus, Leo, Virgo, and Scorpio being known as *Alpasuta* signs.
2. Mars is in the *Lagna,* Saturn is in the 8th, and an *Alpasuta* sign is in the 5th house.
3. Saturn is in the *Lagna,* Jupiter is in the 8th, Mars is in the 12th, and an *Alpasuta* sign is in the 5th house.

Combinations for Unhappiness Through Children: The native will probably not derive any happiness through the children if one of the following combinations is present:

1. Saturn is posited in the 5th house, or the 5th house happens to be a sign owned by Jupiter. This combination is applicable in Leo and Scorpio ascendants.
2. The Moon is in the 5th house in an odd sign or *Navamsha* aspected by the Sun.

Combinations for Adopting a Child: The following planetary combinations indicate that the native may adopt a child:

1. The 5th house is owned by any one of the eunuch planets (Mercury or Saturn), and is aspected by, or conjoined with Saturn. (This combination is possible in Taurus, Aquarius, Virgo, and Libra ascendants).
2. The lord of the 5th house is weak and has no connection with the lords of the 1st and 7th houses.
3. Malefics occupy the 4th or 5th house from the ascendant.
4. Mars is in the 1st house, Saturn in the 8th, and the Sun in the 5th house.
5. Malefics occupy the 8th house from the Moon.

Combinations Leading to Childlessness/Loss of Progeny: Some combinations leading to childlessness or loss of children are enumerated below:

1. Jupiter and the 5th house, counted from the ascendant and the Moon, are aspected by or conjoined with malefic planets.
2. Jupiter and the lords of the 5th house, counted from the ascendant and the Moon, are posited in one or more evil houses, that is, the 6th, 8th, or 12th houses.
3. Jupiter and the 5th house, counted from the ascendant and the Moon, are surrounded on both sides by malefic planets.
4. The Moon is in the 4th house; a malefic planet is in the ascendant; the lord of the ascendant is in the 5th house; and the lord of the 5th house is in the 3rd house.
5. Mars and Saturn aspect the 5th house.
6. The lord of the 5th house and Jupiter are conjoined with Mars.
7. The lord of the 5th house is conjoined with the Sun or Venus.
8. *Rahu* occupies the 5th house, and the lord of the 5th is in an evil house.

9. The lord of the 5th house is conjoined with Mars or *Rahu*.
10. The Sun is in the 1st house, and Mars is in the 5th house.
11. Jupiter occupies the 5th house, and the 5th therefrom is occupied by a malefic planet.
12. The Moon, as lord of the 5th house, combines with Saturn, Mars, or *Rahu*. (The 5th house is owned by the Moon when Pisces is the ascendant.)
13. *Rahu* occupies the 5th house owned by the Moon.
14. The lord of the 5th house is in an inimical or a debilitated sign; or is under combustion; or is in association with the lord of the 6th, 8th, or 12th house, with no benefic aspect or conjunction.
15. The 4th, 7th, and 10th houses are occupied respectively by a malefic planet, Venus, and the Moon.
16. There are malefic planets in the 1st, 5th, 8th, and 12th houses.
17. There is a malefic planet in the 4th house, Jupiter in the 5th, and Venus and Mercury in the 7th house.
18. The Moon is in the 5th house, and malefics in the 1st, 8th, and 12th houses.

Examine Fig. 49 belonging to a native having no children. Note that Jupiter and Mars, as lords of the ascendant and 9th house, respectively, are in the 5th house with Uranus. The Moon, the lord of the 5th house, is under the evil aspect of *Rahu*. Saturn is also aspecting the 5th house as well as its lord, the Moon. Counted from the Moon, the Lord of the 5th house, the Sun, is with *Ketu*, and aspected by *Rahu*.

Combinations to Ascertain the Child's Period of Birth: Children may be born under the following combinations:

1. The major period or sub-period of Jupiter.
2. The major or sub-period of planets ruling the ascendant, the 5th, and the 7th houses.

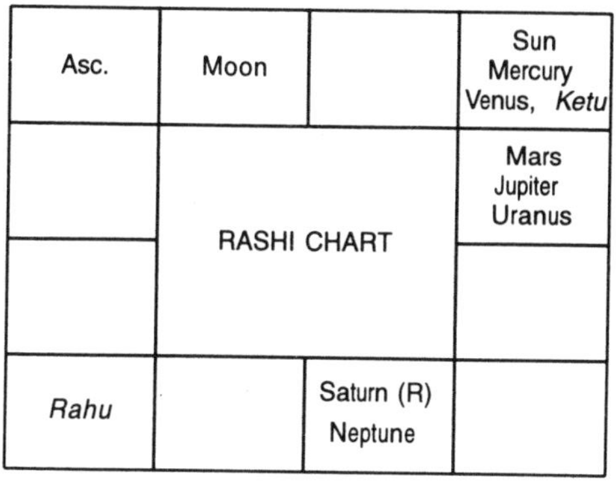

Fig. 49

3. The major or sub-period of planets aspecting the 5th house.
4. Jupiter transits a house which is in the 5th or 9th position from the *Rashi* or *Navamsha* tenanting the 5th house.
5. The lord of the ascendant transits the 5th house, or the sign in which the lord of the 5th is posited.
6. The lord of the ascendant transits its own or exaltation sign; or during transit, conjoins with the lord of the 5th house.

17

Predicting Health, Fitness & Vitality

Diseases are denoted by the 6th house. Planets occupying the 6th house, those aspecting it, the lord of the 6th house, the *Navamsha* occupied by the lord of the 6th house, and the significators of the 6th house (Mars and Saturn) should be considered for predicting the diseases that the native will be prone to. The zodiacal sign in the 6th house signifies the affected part of the body, and its lord signifies the diseases likely to be caused by it. However, it must be understood that each of the planets is capable of causing many a disease when afflicted or ill placed. A strong malefic planet in the 6th house can cause a disease during its period or sub-period.

Aries, Leo, and Sagittarius are fiery signs which govern vitality and control such organs as the head, heart, and thighs. Taurus, Virgo, and Capricorn are earthy signs and control the bones and flesh. Gemini, Libra, and Aquarius are airy signs and govern respiration and the lungs. Cancer, Scorpio, and Pisces are watery signs that rule over the circulatory, digestive, and excretory systems.

The signs of the zodiac representing various diseases are tabulated below.

Sign	*Diseases*
Aries	Brain and eye troubles, fevers
Taurus	Obesity, abscesses, goitre
Gemini	Asthma, rheumatism, consumption
Cancer	Dropsy, smallpox, cancer
Leo	Digestive troubles, diabetes
Virgo	Arthritis, venereal diseases
Libra	Lumbago, kidney stones
Scorpio	Ulcers, fistula, piles
Sagittarius	Gout, paralysis
Capricorn	Leprosy, leucoderma
Aquarius	Diseases of the nervous system
Pisces	Tuberculosis, tumours

Similarly, planets have jurisdiction over certain body parts and the diseases likely to be caused by them.

Planet	*Body Parts Governed by Planets*	*Diseases Likely to be Caused*
The Sun	Head, heart, brain, lungs	High fever, blood pressure, weak eyesight, cerebral disorders
The Moon	Nerves, arteries, veins, brain, uterus, bladder, breast, ovaries, eyes	Catarrh, hysteria, dysentery, dyspepsia, bronchitis, eye troubles, mental aberrations, menstrual disorders
Mars	Marrow, bile, limbs, muscles, blood	High fevers, cuts, burns, haemorrhage, abortion, menstrual disorders, epilepsy
Mercury	Skin, nose, tongue, ears, nervous system	Dumbness, deafness, mental and skin diseases, nasal and urino-genital disorders

Planet	*Body Parts Governed by Planets*	*Diseases Likely to be Caused*
Jupiter	Ears, stomach, intestines, fat	Dropsy, flatulence, abscesses, appendicitis, liver and digestive complaints
Venus	Semen, sex organs, urinary system, face, eyes	Sexual weakness, venereal complaints, spermatorrhoea, leucorrhoea, eye and throat troubles, diabetes
Saturn	Bones, hair, nails	Chronic diseases such as asthma, cancer, tuberculosis, insanity, rheumatism, tooth problems
Rahu and *Ketu*	—	Epilepsy, measles, smallpox, tuberculosis, itches, ulcers, leprosy, insanity

Each house of the zodiac also represents certain parts of the body.

House	*Parts of the Body*
1st house	Head, brain
2nd house	Right eye, throat, neck
3rd house	Hands, shoulders, right ear
4th house	Heart, lungs
5th house	Stomach, liver, intestines
6th house	Kidneys, hips, waist
7th house	Urethra, bladder, uterus, ovaries
8th house	Sex organs
9th house	Thighs
10th house	Knees
11th house	Legs, ankles, left ear
12th house	Feet, toes, left eye

Combinations Leading to Diseases: Combinations responsible for certain diseases are outlined below:

1. Malefics in the 6th house with no benefic aspects cause frequent illness to the native.
2. If the lord of the 6th house occupies an evil house, that is, the 8th or the 12th, the person concerned will suffer from diseases.
3. When the lord of the 11th house is in the 6th house, it causes some complicated disease to the native, as the 6th house is in the 8th position from the 11th house.
4. If the Sun or Saturn and the lord of the 6th house are posited in the *Lagna,* the native will suffer from leprosy.
5. The conjunction of the significators of the 6th house — Mars and Saturn — in the 6th or 12th house causes ulcers and other types of diseases to the native.
6. If the Moon, posited in the 6th, 8th, or the 12th house, is aspected by a malefic, the person concerned will be blind.
7. Saturn in the ascendant, and Mars in the 5th, 7th, or 9th house, cause rheumatism.
8. Mars in the ascendant, aspected by Saturn and the Sun, causes smallpox.
9. When Mercury and the lord of the 6th house are aspected by malefics, they cause deafness.
10. The association of the Moon and Saturn in the 12th house causes insanity to the native. The Moon signifies the mind, and her association with the malefic Saturn in the 12th house is capable of producing a mental disorder.
11. When the Sun, Moon, and Mars together occupy the 6th house, the person concerned suffers from stomach diseases.
12. When Jupiter occupies the 4th house, and is aspected by, or joined with the Sun or Mars, the native suffers from heart diseases.
13. The lords of the 2nd and 3rd house, along with *Rahu,* cause throat complaints.

14. An evil planet in the 3rd house or *Rahu* in the 11th house, and aspected by other evil planets, can cause ear ailments.
15. Venus and Mars together in the 8th house cause diseases of the testicles.
16. Venus occupying the 8th house and aspected by malefics can cause diabetes.
17. When Mars and Venus occupy the 2nd house, they can cause eye diseases.
18. The presence of Jupiter and *Rahu* in the ascendant causes tooth trouble.
19. When Saturn is in the 7th house and aspected by *Rahu,* it may cause urinary troubles. It may be noted that the 7th house in a chart rules over the urethra and bladder.
20. When the Moon or the Sun occupies any watery sign (Cancer, Scorpio, or Pisces), the native is likely to suffer from bronchitis. If Mars is occupying Cancer *Lagna* and is aspected by Saturn (as lord of the 7th and 8th houses), asthma or chronic bronchitis may result.
21. When Mercury and Saturn are situated in the 8th house, impotence may develop in the native. The 8th house rules over the external sex organs, and the presence of two eunuchs (Mercury and Saturn) is enough indication for this malady.
22. If the Sun is in the sign or *Navamsha* of the Moon, and the Moon is in the sign or *Navamsha* of the Sun, the person will suffer from tuberculosis.

The *Rashi* chart of a person who always complained of digestive problems can be seen in Fig. 50. The lord of the 6th house is in an evil house, the 8th. The lord of the 5th house, Saturn, is in the company of a weak Mars which, in turn, is aspecting the 5th house. The ascendant lord, Venus, is in the 12th house, and is aspected by the malefic Jupiter. Reckoned from the Moon, the 6th house is again afflicted by Mars and Saturn.

In Fig. 51, Venus, indicating the eyes, is posited in the house of loss with Uranus. The Moon, another indicator of

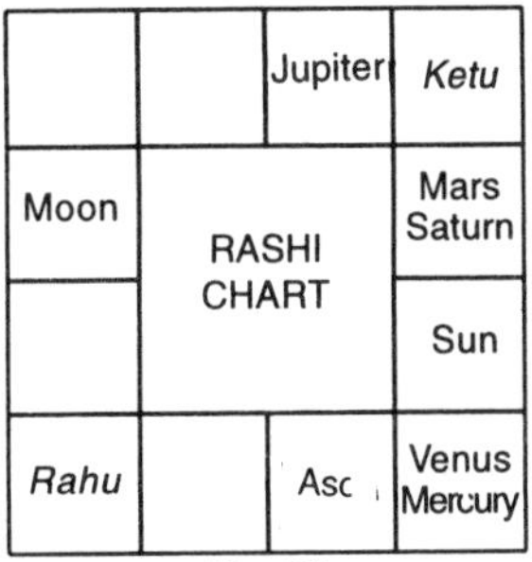

Fig. 50

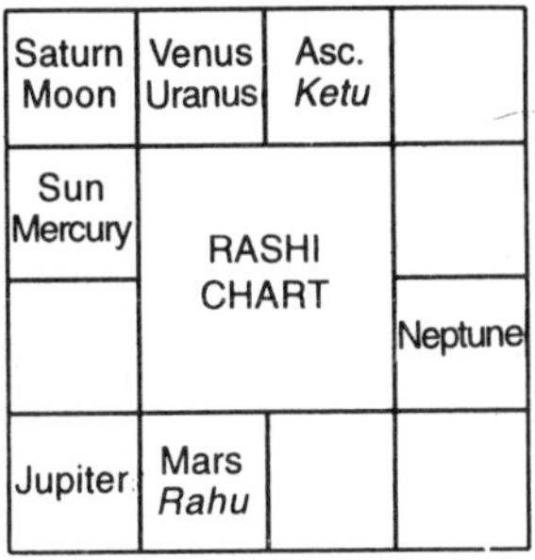

Fig. 51

the eyes, is with Saturn and under the aspect of *Rahu*. The 12th and 2nd house indicate, respectively, the left and the right eye. The lord of the 12th house is with *Rahu*, and the lord of the 2nd house, with the Sun. The 2nd house suffers from the evil aspect of Mars. Due to these combinations the native is likely to have suffered from eye problems and have undergone an operation on both eyes.

18

Predicting Longevity

Longevity is judged from the 8th house, counted both from the ascendant and the Moon. Planets occupying the 8th house, those aspecting it, the lord of the 8th house, the *Navamsha* occupied by the lord of the 8th, and the significator of the 8th house, Saturn, should be considered.

Combinations for a Long Life: A person should have a long life if any of the following combinations is present:

1. Benefic planets are at angles, and malefic planets are present in the *Upachaya* houses (3rd, 6th, and 11th houses).
2. Malefic planets and the lord of the 8th house are in the *Apoklima* houses (3rd, 6th, 9th, and 12th).
3. The lord of the 8th house is in the 8th house.
4. The lords of the ascendant, 8th and 10th houses, and Saturn, are at angles, trines or in the 11th house.
5. The lord of the 8th house is in the ascendant, and is aspected by either Jupiter or Venus.
6. The lord of the 8th house is aspected by or conjoined with Saturn. The role of Saturn in this respect is different. Though a malefic, it increases longevity when placed in the 8th house or when associated with the lord of the 8th house.
7. Both the lord of the ascendant and lord of the 8th house

are posited together in the 8th or 11th house.

8. Saturn is in the 8th house, or the lord of the 8th house is in its own sign.
9. Benefic planets and the lord of the *Lagna* are in *Kendra* houses.
10. The lords of the 1st and 8th houses are in movable signs, or one is in a fixed and the other in a dual sign.
11. The lord of the 6th house is in the 6th or 12th house; and the lord of the 12th is in the 6th, 8th, 12th, or 1st house.
12. The lord of the *lagna* occupies its exaltation sign; the Moon occupies the 11th house; Jupiter, the 8th house.

Study Fig. 47 in Chapter 16 which shows a person with a long life. The lord of the 1st and 8th house, Mars, is strongly placed in a trine. Mars is aspecting the 8th house. The ascendant, the 8th house, and the lord of the ascendant are all aspected by the significator of longevity, Saturn. Saturn itself is powerful in Aquarius in the 11th house, and aspected by Jupiter. The lord of the 6th house is in the 6th house itself. Calculated from the Moon, the lord of the 8th house, Venus, occupies its own sign. All these strong combinations enabled the native to live a disease-free, healthy, and long life.

Combinations for a Short Life: A native will have a short life if any of the following combinations is present:

1. The lord of the 8th house is in the 8th or 12th house along with malefics.
2. The lords of the 8th and 1st houses are in the 6th or 12th house.
3. The lord of the ascendant is a malefic and is posited in the 11th house.
4. The lord of the ascendant occupies the 8th house.
5. Malefic planets are in the 8th house and *Kendras*.
6. A weak Moon, along with malefics, is in the 1st, 5th, 7th, or 9th house.
7. Malefic planets are in the 7th and 8th houses.
8. Malefic planets are in the 1st and 7th houses.

9. Malefic planets are in the 1st and 8th houses.
10. Jupiter is in the 6th, the Moon in the 8th, and Saturn and Mars in the ascendant.
11. Benefic planets and the lord of the *Lagna* occupy the 3rd, 6th, 9th, or 12th house.
12. The lord of the 8th house and malefics are in the *Kendras*.
13. The lords of the 1st and 8th houses are in fixed signs, or, one is in a movable sign, the other, in a dual sign.
14. The ascendant or the Moon is surrounded by malefics.
15. The lord of the ascendant, along with the lord of the 8th house and malefics, occupy the 8th house.
16. A weak moon is positioned in the 6th, 8th, or 12th house.
17. The lord of the 8th house is in its debilitation sign; there are malefics in the 8th house; and the lord of the *Lagna* is weak.

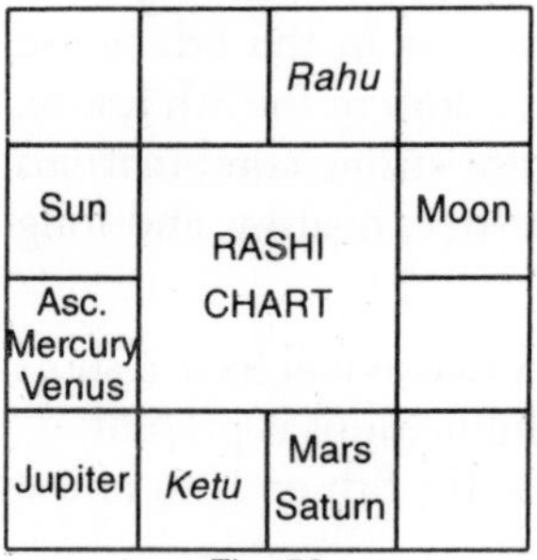

Fig. 52

The *Rashi* chart of a girl who died within a week of her birth can be seen in Fig. 52. The lord of the 8th house occupies an inimical sign, unaspected by benefic planets. The lord of the *Lagna* (Saturn), is in company with another malefic, Mars. The *Lagna* is also aspected by Mars and *Rahu*. The Moon is aspected by Saturn and *Ketu*. Saturn and the Moon are strong and as lords of the 2nd and 7th house, respectively, are acting as death-inflicting planets. Counted from the Moon, the 8th house is occupied by a malefic Sun.

PART THREE

Planetary Influences

19

Dasha: The Ruling Period of a Planet

The *Dasha* of a planet refers to the ruling period of that planet. *Dashas* are the periods during which good or bad effects of the planets are felt by an individual. The *Dasha* or effect of a planet is interrelated with the native's past *Karmas* or actions. Various *Dashas* and their sequence depend upon the longitude and sign in which the Moon is placed at the native's birth. Favourable *Dashas* bring good luck to the native concerned, while unfavourable *Dashas* bring misfortune and troubles. Therefore it is necessary to calculate the *Dashas* so as to find out the timing of various events in the life of an individual.

Various *Dasha* systems are followed by different astrologers. However, the *Vimshottari Dasha* system is the most widely accepted as it has been found to yield satisfactory results. According to this system, the span of human life is taken to be of 120 years. This period of 120 years is distributed among the 9 planets, with each planet being assigned to a fixed number of years.

The planetary *Dashas* always operate in the following order:

Planet	*Assigned Period in years*
The Sun	6
The Moon	10
Mars	7
Rahu	18
Jupiter	16
Saturn	19
Mercury	17
Ketu	7
Venus	20

The *Dasha* of each planet has sub-periods which follow exactly the same order as given above.

Suppose the *Dasha* of the Sun is in progress. The first sub-period will be that of the Sun, the next will be that of the Moon, followed by Mars, *Rahu*, Jupiter, Saturn, Mercury, *Ketu*, and Venus.

Sun's Period-6 Years Sub-periods

	Sun	*Mo-on*	*Mars*	*Rahu*	*Jup-iter*	*Sat-urn*	*Mer-cury*	*Ketu*	*Venus*	*To-tal*
Years	0	0	0	0	0	0	0	0	1	6
Months	3	6	4	10	9	11	10	4	0	
Days	18	0	6	24	18	12	6	6	0	

Moon's Period-10 Years Sub-periods

	Mo-on	*Mars*	*Rahu*	*Jup-iter*	*Sat-urn*	*Mer-cury*	*Ketu*	*Venus*	*Sun*	*To-tal*
Years	0	0	1	1	1	1	0	1	0	10
Months	10	7	6	4	7	5	7	8	6	
Days	0	0	0	0	0	0	0	0	0	

Mars' Period-7 Years Sub-periods

	Mars	*Rahu*	*Jupiter*	*Saturn*	*Mercury*	*Ketu*	*Venus*	*Sun*	*Moon*	*Total*
Years	0	1	0	1	0	0	1	0	0	7
Months	4	0	11	1	11	4	2	4	7	
Days	27	18	6	9	27	27	0	6	0	

Rahu's **Period-18 Years Sub-periods**

	Rahu	*Jupiter*	*Saturn*	*Mercury*	*Ketu*	*Venus*	*Sun*	*Moon*	*Mars*	*Total*
Years	2	2	2	2	1	3	0	1	1	18
Months	8	4	10	6	0	0	10	6	0	
Days	12	24	6	18	18	0	24	0	18	

Jupiter's Period-16 Years Sub-periods

	Jupiter	*Saturn*	*Mercury*	*Ketu*	*Venus*	*Sun*	*Moon*	*Mars*	*Rahu*	*Total*
Years	2	2	2	0	2	0	1	0	2	16
Months	1	6	3	11	8	9	4	11	4	
Days	18	12	6	6	0	18	0	6	24	

Saturn's Period-19 Years Sub-periods

	Saturn	*Mercury*	*Ketu*	*Venus*	*Sun*	*Moon*	*Mars*	*Rahu*	*Jupiter*	*Total*
Years	3	2	1	3	0	1	1	2	2	19
Months	0	8	1	2	11	7	1	10	6	
Days	3	9	9	0	12	0	9	6	12	

Mercury's Period-17 Years Sub-periods

	Mercury	*Ketu*	*Venus*	*Sun*	*Moon*	*Mars*	*Rahu*	*Jupiter*	*Saturn*	*Total*
Years	2	0	2	0	1	0	2	2	2	17
Months	4	11	10	10	5	11	6	3	8	
Days	27	27	0	6	0	27	18	6	9	

Ketu's Period-7 Years Sub-periods

	Ketu	*Venus*	*Sun*	*Moon*	*Mars*	*Rahu*	*Jupiter*	*Saturn*	*Mercury*	*Total*
Years	0	1	0	0	0	1	0	1	0	7
Months	4	2	4	7	4	0	11	1	11	
Days	27	0	6	0	27	18	6	9	27	

Venus' Period-20 Years Sub-periods

	Venus	*Sun*	*Moon*	*Mars*	*Rahu*	*Jupiter*	*Saturn*	*Mercury*	*Ketu*	*Total*
Years	3	1	1	1	3	2	3	2	1	20
Months	4	0	8	2	0	8	2	10	2	
Days	0	0	0	0	0	0	0	0	0	

The sub-periods of each planet are further divided into minor sub-periods. (These have been omitted from the book for the sake of simplicity).

Calculation of *Dashas*

1. Calculate the balance of Dasha in force for a native born on October 1, 1968 at 3.25 a.m. in Neemuch, Madhya Pradesh.

For the calculation of the running *Dasha* and its remaining period at the birth of a native, we must know the longitude of the Moon at that time. The Moon's longitude was found out to be 6°- 26' in the sign Capricorn. Now note the period from the Table of Balance of *Vimshottari Dasha* (see p. 132) against 6° from the column 'Moon in Capricorn'. The period mentioned is 1 year, 9 months, 18 days of the Sun. Substract from it the period for 26 minutes (calculated with the help of the Table of Proportional Parts for *Dasha* of Planets — see p. 133). The total period for 26 minutes from the Sun's column comes to 2 months, 10 days.

	Yr.		Mo.		D.
	1	-	9	-	18
(-)		-	2	-	10
	1	-	7	-	8

The balance of the Sun's *Dasha,* therefore, at the time of the birth of the native was 1 year, 7 months, and 8 days. This was the remaining period of the Sun to be enjoyed by the native in the present birth.

2. Find out the sequence of various Dashas to be enjoyed by the native.

Add the balance of the Sun's *Dasha* (1yr. 7mo. 8d.) to the date of birth of the native.

	Yr.	-	Mo.	-	D.	
	1968	-	10	-	1	
(+)	1	-	7	-	8	
	1970	-	5	-	9	Sun

This illustrates that the Sun's *Dasha* was in force up to May 9, 1970. The Sun's *Dasha* will be followed next by the Moon (10 years), then Mars (7 years), *Rahu* (18 years), Jupiter (16 years), Saturn (19 years), and so on.

	Yr.	-	Mo.	-	D.	
	1970	-	5	-	9	
(+)	10					
	1980	-	5	-	9	Moon
(+)	7	-				
	1987	-	5	-	9	Mars
(+)	18	-				
	2005	-	5	-	9	*Rahu*
(+)	16	-				
	2021	-	5	-	9	Jupiter
(+)	19	-				
	2040	-	5	-	9	Saturn

3. Calculate various sub-periods in the Moon's Dasha of the native.

The Moon's *Dasha* (10 years) of the native was in operation from May 9, 1970 to May 9, 1980. Therefore, various sub-periods in the Moon's *Dasha* will be as under:

	Yr.	-	Mo.	-	D.	
	1970	-	5	-	9	
(+)	0	-	10	-	0	
	1971	-	3	-	9	Moon in Moon
(+)	0	-	7	-	0	
	1971	-	10	-	9	Mars in Moon
(+)	1	-	6	-	0	
	1973	-	4	-	9	*Rahu* in Moon
(+)	1	-	4	-	0	
	1974	-	8	-	9	Jupiter in Moon
(+)	1	-	7	-	0	
	1976	-	3	-	9	Saturn in Moon
(+)	1	-	5	-	0	
	1977	-	8	-	9	Mercury in Moon
(+)	0	-	7	-	0	
	1978	-	3	-	9	*Ketu* in Moon
(+)	1	-	8	-	0	
	1979	-	11	-	9	Venus in Moon
(+)	0	-	6	-	0	
	1980	-	5	-	9	Sun in Moon

Balance of *Vimshottari Dasha* by Longitude of the Moon

Degrees	*Moon in Aries, Leo, Sagittarius*			*Moon in Taurus, Virgo, Capricorn*			*Moon in Gemini, Libra, Aquarius*			*Moon in Cancer, Scorpio, Pisces*		
	Yr.	*Mo.*	*D.*	*Yr.*	*Mo.*	*D.*	*Yr*	*Mo.*	*D.*	*Yr.*	*Mo.*	*D.*
	Ketu			Sun			Mars			Jupiter		
1	6	5	21	4	0	18	2	11	21	2	9	18
2	5	11	12	3	7	6	2	5	12	1	7	6
3	5	5	3	3	1	24	1	11	3	0	4	24
										Saturn		
4	4	10	24	2	8	12	1	4	24	18	0	18
5	4	4	15	2	3	0	0	10	15	16	7	15
6	3	10	6	1	9	18	0	4	6	15	2	12
							Rahu					
7	3	3	27	1	4	6	17	6	18	13	9	9
8	2	9	18	0	10	24	16	2	12	12	4	6
9	2	3	9	0	5	12	14	10	6	10	11	3
				Moon								
10	1	9	0	10	0	0	13	6	0	9	6	0
11	1	2	21	9	3	0	12	1	24	8	0	27
12	0	8	12	8	6	0	10	9	18	6	7	24
13	0	2	3	7	9	0	9	5	12	5	2	21
	Venus											
14	19	0	0	7	0	0	8	1	6	3	9	18
15	17	6	0	6	3	0	6	9	0	2	4	15
16	16	0	0	5	6	0	5	4	24	0	11	12
										Mercury		
17	14	6	0	4	9	0	4	0	18	16	6	27
18	13	0	0	4	0	0	2	8	12	15	3	18
19	11	6	0	3	3	0	1	4	6	14	0	9
							Jupiter					
20	10	0	0	2	6	0	16	0	0	12	9	0
21	8	6	0	1	9	0	14	9	18	11	5	21
22	7	0	0	1	0	0	13	7	6	10	2	12
23	5	6	0	0	3	0	12	4	24	8	11	3
				Mars								
24	4	0	0	6	7	24	11	2	12	7	7	24
25	2	6	0	6	1	15	10	0	0	6	4	15
26	1	0	0	5	7	6	8	9	18	5	1	6
	Sun											
27	5	10	6	5	0	27	7	7	6	3	9	27
28	5	4	24	4	6	18	6	4	24	2	6	18
29	4	11	12	4	0	9	5	2	12	1	3	9
30	4	6	0	3	6	0	4	0	0	0	0	0

Proportional Parts for *Dasha* of Planets

Minutes	*Ketu*		Venus		Sun		Moon		Mars		*Rahu*		Jupiter		Saturn		Mercury	
	Mo.	D.	Mo.	D.	Mo.	D.	Mo.	D.	Mo.	D.	Mo.	D.	Mo.	D.	Mo.	D.	Mo.	D.
1	0	3	0	9	0	3	0	5	0	3	0	8	0	7	0	9	0	8
2	0	6	0	18	0	5	0	9	0	6	0	16	0	14	0	17	0	15
3	0	9	0	27	0	8	0	14	0	9	0	24	0	22	0	26	0	23
4	0	13	1	6	0	11	0	18	0	13	1	2	0	29	1	4	1	1
5	0	16	1	15	0	14	0	23	0	16	1	11	1	6	1	13	1	8
6	0	19	1	24	0	16	0	27	0	19	1	19	1	13	1	21	1	16
7	0	22	2	3	0	19	1	2	0	22	1	27	1	20	2	0	1	24
8	0	25	2	12	0	22	1	6	0	25	2	5	1	28	2	8	2	1
9	0	28	2	21	0	24	1	11	0	28	2	13	2	5	2	17	2	9
10	1	1	3	0	0	27	1	15	1	1	2	21	2	12	2	26	2	17
15	1	17	4	15	1	11	2	8	1	17	4	2	3	18	4	8	3	25
20	2	3	6	0	1	24	3	0	2	3	5	12	4	24	5	21	5	3

Effects of *Dashas*

Each planet exercises a good or bad effect during the main period or sub-periods of its *Dasha*. These effects depend on whether the planet is favourably disposed or otherwise to the native.

The Sun — Main Period: If the Sun is well-placed, his *Dasha* will bestow prosperity, power, happiness, wisdom, and fame on the native. If the Sun is in an inauspicious position, the native may suffer hardships, face the displeasure of superiors, and encounter troubles through enemies and diseases. There may be loss of money and position. The health of the native's father may be adversely affected.

Sub-periods:

The Sun	Sickness, anxiety, loss of money, travels, misunderstanding and unpleasantness with relatives and superiors
The Moon	Monetary gains, land and ornaments, eye troubles, destruction of enemies
Mars	Mental worries, quarrels, diseases, failures, gain or loss of money
Rahu	Loss of money, many troubles, family disputes, scandals
Jupiter	Gains in education, wealth and position, virtuous acts, benefits from friends, birth of a child
Saturn	Heavy expenditure, sickness of family members, unhappiness and mental worries, accidents, quarrels with relatives
Mercury	A good reputation, excellent earnings, ill health, mental worries, fruitless travels
Ketu	Disputes with friends, loss of position and money, quarrels, change of residence, danger from enemies
Venus	Monetary gains, acquisition of a vehicle, marriage, illness, association with bad women

The Moon — Main Period: When the Moon is in a favourable position, the person concerned will procure wealth, a wife, land, and royal favours. In other words, there will be all-round prosperity and success. If however, the Moon is weak, the native will face mental troubles and other sufferings, including trouble to his mother.

Sub-periods:

The Moon	Good health, worthy reputation, power and prosperity, birth of a child, conjugal happiness
Mars	Loss of wealth and honour, hardships, quarrels, diseases, trouble from enemies
Rahu	Diseases, loss of money, enmity with superiors and relatives, scandals, mental worries
Jupiter	Monetary gains, property, comforts and happiness, success in undertakings, birth of a child, favours from superiors, religious acts
Saturn	Loss of property and health, mental worries, illness of wife and children, quarrels with friends
Mercury	Increase of wealth and happiness, intellectual achievements, honour from superiors
Ketu	Loss of relatives, illness of wife, monetary losses, eye troubles, danger to parents and children, dishonour
Venus	Acquisition of money and articles of luxury, sickness, marriage, birth of a child, improvement in business or profession
The Sun	Travels, loss of money, destruction of enemies, honour from superiors, end of a disease

Mars — Main Period: When Mars is placed in an auspicious position, his benevolence will bring wealth, knowledge, land, and other desired objects to the native. If

Mars is in an inauspicious position, the native will be surrounded with troubles, quarrels and misunderstandings, litigations, association with low women, danger from fire, wounds, and diseases.

Sub-periods:

Mars	Failure in undertakings, trouble with superiors, quarrels with relatives, loss of money
Rahu	Skin diseases, loss of money, danger from weapons, enemies and thieves, loss of relatives, scandals
Jupiter	Favours from superiors, birth of a child, monetary gains, good reputation and happiness
Saturn	Quarrels and troubles; loss of money, property, and position; diseases, intense grief
Mercury	Gain and loss of money and knowledge, mental worries, trouble from enemies and thieves
Ketu	Loss of money, many enemies, sinful acts, family disputes
Venus	Acquisition of money and happiness, favourable associations, love affairs, skin eruptions
The Sun	Good reputation, monetary gains, diseases, many enemies, honour from or trouble through persons in high positions
The Moon	Gain of wealth, birth of a child, illness of elders, various types of enjoyment

***Rahu* — Main Period**: During the period of a favourable *Rahu*, the native will enjoy all-round prosperity and a position of authority. The native will be well reputed, and happy and successful in his undertakings. The unfavourable *Rahu*, on the other hand, will create all sorts of troubles, disease, and misunderstanding. The native's children and wife may suffer from illness and the death of relatives may take place.

Sub-periods:

Rahu	Loss of friends, trouble from harmful persons, scandals, loss of money, mental worries, illness of wife, quarrels with near and dear ones
Jupiter	Destruction of enemies, acquisition of wealth, birth of a child, success in efforts, sound health, happiness
Saturn	Loss of position, quarrels, scandals, bad associations, diseases
Mercury	Gain of wealth and favours, birth of a child, help from friends
Ketu	Ill health of children, quarrels with friends, loss of money and honour, all types of hardship and suffering
Venus	Birth of a child, marriage, conjugal happiness, trouble from enemies and diseases
The Sun	Eye disease, a good reputation and fame, mental worries, change of job or residence, sickness of family members
The Moon	Quarrels, mental agony, loss of money, change of job or residence, loss or danger to wife and children
Mars	Loss of money and position, disputes and worries, trouble with superiors, danger of theft, eye disease

Jupiter — Main Period: An auspicious Jupiter blesses the native with children, wealth, and prosperity. The native will receive fame and honour and will be successful in his undertakings. An inauspicious Jupiter brings in increased expenditure, ear disease, phlegmatic disorders, and death of parents or other elders.

Sub-periods:

Jupiter	Step-up in income and reputation, favours from superiors and happiness, birth of a child, success in all attempts

Saturn	Failure in attempts, problems for wife and children, heavy expenditure, mental worries, rise in status
Mercury	Increased income, happiness and material comforts, birth of a child, favour from superiors
Ketu	Sufferings, illness, loss of money, problems for children and wife, separation from relatives and friends
Venus	Acquisition of luxurious articles, money and fame, auspicious activities, marital happiness, peace of mind, success in profession or business
The Sun	Sound health, increase in income, favours from superiors, happiness, comfortable life
The Moon	Increase in income, fame and prosperity, destruction of enemies, birth of a child, auspicious activities
Mars	Various kinds of loss and disappointment; failure in undertakings; acquisition of money, fame, and land; mental agony
Rahu	Loss of money; all sorts of suffering, sickness, intense mental agony; trouble from the government and enemies

Saturn — Main Period: If Saturn is favourable, its period will prove beneficial and prosperous. The native will become famous and shine in his career. When Saturn is unfavourable, there will be loss of wealth and happiness, combined with trouble to the native or his wife or children.

Sub-periods:

Saturn	Loss of money, ill health in the entire family, disputes with and troubles from relatives, laziness, sinful activities
Mercury	Monetary gains and general prosperity, birth of a child, happiness and fame, favours from superiors

Ketu	Sickness, suffering, quarrels in the family, enmity, loss of money
Venus	Profit in business or profession, birth of a child, company of friends, general happiness, favours from superiors
The Sun	Sickness of wife and children, eye complaints, danger from enemies, loss of money
The Moon	Troubles and sickness, loss of money, death of a near relative, quarrels with friends and relatives
Mars	Loss of money or position, change of residence, illness, serious quarrels and enmity
Rahu	sickness, increase in troubles and enemies, bodily injuries, loss of money
Jupiter	Increase in wealth, position, and material comforts; happy family life; fulfilment of desires; religious activities

Mercury — Main Period: If Mercury is favourable, it will confer fame, happiness, money, position, and knowledge on the native. If it is unfavourable, the native will lose money and land. He may suffer from ailments caused by the three humours. The native will encounter misunderstanding and troubles with his relatives and friends.

Sub-periods:

Mercury	Success in all undertakings, birth of a child, advance in profession, increase in knowledge, help from superiors
Ketu	Disease, grief, quarrels, loss of money or property, failure in certain attempts, mental agony
Venus	Acquisition of money, jewels and clothes; birth of a child; happy married life; many gains; marriage
The Sun	Help from persons in a favourable position, troubles from enemies, sickness of wife, monetary gains, many obstacles

The Moon	Various ailments leading to ill health or physical injuries, success and happiness
Mars	Favours from influential people, end of some disease, destruction of enemies, quarrels, loss of position, fear, rheumatic pain
Rahu	Loss of wealth, skin diseases, sickness, humiliation, disputes and failures
Jupiter	Acquisition of land and wealth, worthy reputation, happiness, birth of a child, marriage, favour from superiors, religious deeds
Saturn	Scandals, troubles, loss of money, unsuccessful undertakings, enmity, fear and anxiety, diseases

***Ketu* — Main Period**: If *Ketu* is in a favourable position, the native will achieve success in all his undertakings, gain money, and destroy his enemies. However, when *Ketu* is unfavourably placed, it will burden the native with fruitless efforts, intense misery, humiliation, trouble from enemies, loss of money, and various ailments.

Sub-periods:

Ketu	Quarrels and misunderstandings, loss of wealth and happiness, mental worries, separation from relatives
Venus	Birth of a child, misunderstanding with or illness of wife, quarrels, humiliation
The Sun	Illness, disappointments, obstacles in undertakings, hostility of relatives and friends
The Moon	Sudden gain or loss of money, mental agony
Mars	Fear and anxiety, family quarrels, enmity and disputes, losses and obstacles
Rahu	Undesirable acts; loss of money, property and honour; trouble from superiors; fear and anxiety

Jupiter	Birth of a child, marriage, gain of land, money and honour, profit in business
Saturn	Trouble from enemies, heavy expenditure, loss of status, change of residence, mental worries, illness of spouse
Mercury	Acquisition of knowledge, wealth, and lands; anxiety; trouble from enemies

Venus — Main period: A favourable Venus exudes happiness, prosperity, high status, various type of gains, conjugal happiness, and intellectual pursuits. When Venus is unfavourable, trouble will beset the native's wife; the native, in time, will face mental anguish and witness the death of elders. Additionally, he will lose money, commit faults, and suffer from diseases.

Sub-periods:

Venus	Many pleasures, birth of a child, active sex life, monetary gains, success in efforts
The Sun	Ailments relating to the eyes and head, quarrels with wife and family members, anxiety, fear
The Moon	Gain in wealth and articles of luxury, accomplishment of desires, diseases
Mars	Acquisition of money and property, eye and venereal diseases, active sex life
Rahu	Many quarrels, recovery of lost property, danger of fire, thieves and poisoning, seclusion
Jupiter	Procurement of knowledge, happiness, fame, and health; increased income; conjugal happiness
Saturn	Gain of money, honour, and property; destruction of enemies; loss of money; immoral acts; ill health
Mercury	Increase in income, knowledge, fame, and happiness; favours from superiors; happiness through wife and children

Ketu	Loss of happiness and money, illness of spouse, injuries, sorrows

Judging the Results of a *Dasha*

There are certain combinations which determine whether the effect of a *Dasha* will be benefic or malefic.

1. The *Dasha* of a planet will be favourable if its lord is in its own, friendly, or exaltation sign; is associated with or aspected by a benefic planet; owns the 1st, 4th, 5th, 9th, or 10th house from the ascendant.
2. The *Dasha* of a planet will be unfavourable if its lord is in an inimical or debilitation sign, or is combust by the Sun; is associated with or aspected by a malefic planet; owns the 3d, 6th, 8th, 11th, or 12th house from the ascendant.
3. The *Dasha* of the lord of the ascendant will bring prosperity and happiness to the native.
4. The *Dasha* of the lord of the 2d house will provide monetary gains but little happiness.
5. Favourable results will not be felt by the native during the *Dasha* of the lord of the 3d house.
6. The native will get happiness, landed property/house, and comforts during the *Dasha* of the lord of the 4th house.
7. The native will receive education, and be blessed with children during the *Dasha* of the lord of the 5th house.
8. There will be enmity and misunderstanding during the *Dasha* of the lord of the 6th house.
9. The *Dasha* of the 7th lord will give both sorrow and happiness to the native.
10. During the *Dasha* of the 8th lord, harmful effects will be felt by the native.
11. The *Dasha* of the lord of the 9th house will prove fortunate. The native may perform religious functions and charitable acts during this period.
12. The *Dasha* of the lord of the 10th house will enhance monetary gains and the native's career.

13. The native will experience gains and losses during the *Dasha* of the lord of the 11th house.
14. During the *Dasha* of the lord of the 12th house, troubles and losses will beset the native.
15. Planets in Leo, Virgo, Libra, Scorpio, and Aquarius will produce good results at the beginning of their *Dashas*; in Gemini and Pisces — in the middle of their *Dashas;* and in Aries, Taurus, Cancer, Sagittarius, and Capricorn — at the end of their *Dashas.*
16. Benefic planets, if debilitated or in inimical signs, will produce evil results.
17. Benefic planets in exaltation and malefic planets in debilitation will produce good results.
18. A planet occupying an exaltation sign but debilitated in *Navamsha*, or debilitated in the sign but exalted in *Navamsha*, will produce mixed results.
19. Good or evil results produced by planets in their main and sub-periods will depend on whether they are benefic or malefic towards the native.
20. Planets in their main periods will produce results according to their ownership of the houses.
21. Planets in their sub-periods will produce results based on their occupation of different houses.
22. During the *Dasha* of a favourable planet, the sub-period of another favourable planet will produce good results.
23. During the *Dasha* of a favourable planet, the sub-period of an unfavourable planet will produce mixed results.
24. During the *Dasha* of an unfavourable planet, the sub-period of a favourable planet will produce mixed results.
25. During the *Dasha* of an unfavourable planet, the sub-period of another unfavourable planet will produce evil results.
26. In the main period of a planet, the sub-period of a friendly planet will produce good results; that of an inimical planet will produce evil results; and that of a neutral planet will produce mixed results.

27. In a particular *Dasha*, results of sub-periods will be modified as below by the effect of the transit of planets:

    The sub-period of a favourable planet + favourable transit will produce good results.

    The sub-period of a favourable planet + unfavourable transit will produce mixed results.

    The sub-period of an unfavourable planet + favourable transit will produce mixed results.

    The sub-period of an unfavourable planet + unfavourable transit will produce evil results.
28. The *Dasha* of a *Yogakaraka* planet will produce good results.
29. The *Dasha* of a *Vargottama* planet (occupying the same *Rashi* and *Navamsha)* will produce good results.
30. During the *Dasha* of a planet, the sub-period of the planet occupying the 6th, 8th, or 12th sign from the main *Dasha* lord will produce unfavourable results.
31. Saturn's *Dasha* will prove unfavourable if it happens to be the 4th in order from the *Dasha* operating at the time of birth. Similarly, the *Dasha* of Jupiter will prove unfavourable if it happens to be the 6th, and of Mars and *Rahu,* if 5th in the order.
32. The *Dasha* of *Rahu* or *Ketu* will produce good results if posited in a *Kendra* or *Trikona* house, and if aspected by or associated with benefic planets. Similar results will be obtained if *Rahu* or *Ketu* is associated with the lord of the sign it occupies.

20

Planets in Transit: Benefic and Malefic Effects

The transit or *Gochara* means the movement of planets through various houses of the zodiac counted from the Moon. The transit results supplement the *Dasha* indications and are, thus, very important for predictive purposes. While passing through various houses, the planets produce good or bad effects, depending on whether they are benefic or malefic in a particular chart. In the transit system, the counting is done from the sign or *Rashi* in which the Moon is posited, that is, the *Janma Rashi*. The *Janma Rashi* (natal Moon) refers to the position of the Moon at the time of birth, while the *Lagna* (ascendant) refers to the rising sign at the time of birth. Houses are counted from the *Janma Rashi* in the same manner as from the *Lagna*. Suppose, in a horoscope, the *Janma Rashi* is Capricorn. Now if Jupiter transits the sign Cancer, then this may be treated as the transit of Jupiter in the 7th house from the *Janma Rashi*. Similarly, Saturn's transit through the sign Capricorn may be taken as the transit of Saturn through the 1st house from the *Janma Rashi*.

The sun produces good results when he transits through the 3rd, 6th, 10th, and 11th houses from the Moon. The Moon showers good effects only when she passes through the 1st, 3rd, 6th, 7th, 10th, and 11th positions from herself. Mercury is benefic in the 2nd, 4th, 6th, 8th, 10th, and 11th places. Mars, Saturn, *Rahu*, and *Ketu* produce positive results in the 3rd, 6th, and 11th houses from the Moon. Jupiter is benefic in the 2nd, 5th, 7th, 9th, and 11th places; and Venus is favourable in the 1st, 2nd, 3rd, 4th, 5th, 8th, 9th, 11th, and 12th places from the Moon.

It should be remembered that the Sun and Mars produce some effects when they pass through the first 10° of a sign. Jupiter and Venus are effectual between 10° - 20°; the Moon and Saturn between 20° - 30°; and Mercury and *Rahu* throughout their transit in a sign.

Rules Governing Transits

1. A planet in transit through its exaltation, own, or friendly sign produces good results. In an inimical or debilitation sign it produces bad results.
2. A planet in transit in its exaltation, own, or friendly sign, but passing through an unfavourable house, will produce mixed results.
3. While moving through a favourable house, if a planet is surrounded by malefics from both sides, its good effects will be nullified.
4. The good effects of transit will also not be felt if a planet in transit gets into *Vedha*.
5. The good effects of transit will be increased if a planet is aspected by or is associated with another benefic planet during its transit.
6. While passing through the houses, those planets which have more than 4 benefic crossmarks in their *Ashtakavarga* produce favourable results despite their moving through unfavourable houses counted from the *Janma Rashi*.
7. Good results will be bestowed on the native if there is a benefic planet in the 4th, 5th, 8th, or 9th house, counted from a planet moving through a favourable place.
8. Planets do not produce good results even when they transit through favourable places counted from the Moon, if they are simultaneously eclipsed by the Sun's

rays. The Moon, Mars, Mercury, Jupiter, Venus, and Saturn get eclipsed within 12°, 17°, 14°, 11°, 10°, and 15°, respectively from the Sun.

9. There will be loss of money and honour if Saturn transits through the 1st house, Jupiter through the 3rd, Mercury through the 4th, the Sun through the 5th, Venus through the 6th, Mars through the 7th, the Moon through the 8th, and *Rahu* through the 9th house, counted from the *Janma Rashi*.
10. The Sun, Mars, Jupiter, and Saturn, while passing through the 1st, 8th, and 12th houses, produce danger to the life of the native. He will suffer a loss of position and money. The transit of Saturn through the 1st, 2nd, and 12th houses from the Moon is called Saturn's *Sade Sati*, which proves bad in all respects.

Vedha

Vedha or places of obstruction should be taken into consideration while predicting transit results through various signs. The benefic transit of a planet can be obstructed or nullified when another planet moves into a specific place. For example, the Sun's transit is favourable in the 3rd house when counted from the Moon. If any other planet transits the 9th house from the Moon, it will have an obstructive effect, and the benefits of the Sun's transit will not be felt by the native. The converse is also true; that is, if the Sun is moving through the 9th house, and if there is another planet moving in the 3rd house, *Vedha* will occur. It should be noted, however, that there is no *Vedha* between the Sun and Saturn, and between Mercury and the Moon.

The *Vedha* positions, as well as the houses where the benefic transit of the planets occurs, are given in the following table. The favourable transit positions of the Sun are 3, 6, 10, and 11. His corresponding *Vedha* positions are 9, 12, 4, and 5. For the Moon, the benefic houses of transit are 1, 3, 6, 7, 10, and 11. Her corresponding *Vedha* positions are 5, 9, 12, 2, 4, and 8.

Planets	*Houses of benefic transit*	*Corresponding Vedha positions*
The Sun	3, 6, 10, 11	9, 12, 4, 5
The Moon	1, 3, 6, 7, 10, 11	5, 9, 12, 2, 4, 8
Mars	3, 6, 11	12, 9, 5
Mercury	2, 4, 6, 8, 10, 11	5, 3, 9, 1, 7, 12
Jupiter	2, 5, 7, 9, 11	12, 4, 3, 10, 8
Venus	1, 2, 3, 4, 5, 8, 9, 10, 12	8, 7, 1, 10, 9, 5, 11, 6, 3
Saturn	3, 6, 11	12, 9, 5

Transit Through Various *Nakshatras*

In this method the *Nakshatra* of the Moon at the time of birth (Natal Star or *Janma Nakshatra)* is taken into consideration. The counting of the *Nakshatra* is done from the *Janma Nakshatra* of the native. For example, if the *Janma Nakshatra* is *Uttarabhadrapada*, the counting will be done by taking *Uttarabhadrapada* as 1, *Revati* as 2, *Ashwini* as 3, *Bharani* as 4, and so on.

1. The Sun is benefic when he transits through the 2nd, 4th, 6th, 8th, 9th, 11th, 13th, and 24th *Nakshatras* reckoned from the *Janma Nakshatra.*
2. The Moon has a good effect when she transits through the 4th, 6th, 8th, 9th, 11th, 13th, 15th, 26th, and 27th *Nakshatras.*
3. The transit of Mars through the 9th, 11th, 17th, 22nd, and 24th *Nakshatras* is favourable.
4. Mercury, Jupiter, and Venus are benefic when they transit through the 4th, 6th, 13th, 15th, 17th, 20th, 22nd, 24th, 26th, and 27th *Nakshatras.*
5. Saturn, *Rahu* and *Ketu* are benefic in the 2nd, 4th, 6th, 8th, 13th, 15th, 17th, 18th, 20th, 22nd, and 24th *Nakshatras.*

Effects of Transit

The effects of transit or *Gochara* of the planets through the twelve houses, counted from the sign occupied by the Moon at birth, are as follows:

The Sun:

1st House	Loss of money, obstacles in undertakings, illness
2nd House	Loss of money, quarrels, unhappiness
3rd House	Promotion, happiness, good health, increase in income
4th House	Domestic unhappiness, ill health, quarrels, financial worries
5th House	Mental worries, ill health of children
6th House	Happiness, gains, success in undertakings
7th House	Anxiety, diseases
8th House	Diseases, quarrels, heavy expenditure
9th House	Humiliation, grief, enmity
10th House	Gains, success in undertakings
11th House	Promotion, monetary gains, domestic happiness, success in undertakings
12th House	Loss of money, quarrels, grief

The Moon:

1st House	Gains, rise in fortune, sexual pleasures
2nd House	Loss of money, obstacles, disputes
3rd House	Success, monetary gains, happiness
4th House	Fear, anxiety, loss of money, domestic unhappiness
5th House	Illness, sorrow, obstacles in undertakings
6th House	Monetary gains, good health, happiness
7th House	Monetary gains, all-round happiness
8th House	Troubles, quarrels, untoward events
9th House	Troubles from enemies, diseases
10th House	Success, happiness, gains
11th House	Prosperity, happiness, good health
12th House	Expenditure and loss of money, accidents, a misunderstanding

Mars:

1st House	Loss of money, obstacles in undertakings, sickness

2nd House	Increase in expenditure, loss, quarrels
3rd House	Good health, monetary gains, happiness, success
4th House	Loss of position, illness, domestic unhappiness
5th House	Quarrels, ill health of children, enmity, loss
6th House	Success, gains, good health
7th House	Eye and stomach diseases, domestic quarrels, loss
8th House	Illness, loss of money, mental worries
9th House	Loss of money, humiliation, physical weakness
10th House	Loss of money, ill health, obstacles
11th House	Money and property, success, domestic happiness, birth of a child
12th House	Heavy expenditure, quarrels, losses

Mercury:

1st House	Quarrels, losses, enmity
2nd House	Dishonour, scandals, misery, success
3rd House	Enmity, troubles, loss of money
4th House	General prosperity, happiness
5th House	Quarrels with wife and children
6th House	Success in undertakings, prosperity, domestic happiness
7th House	Misery, obstacles, quarrels, illness
8th House	Increase in income, happiness and power, birth of a child
9th House	Loss of money, enmity, obstacles
10th House	All-round success and happiness
11th House	Happiness and prosperity, birth of a child
12th House	Troubles, diseases, loss of money, domestic quarrels

Jupiter:

1st House	Sickness, loss of money, worries
2nd House	Increase in income, happiness and success, birth of a child
3rd House	Loss of money, friends, and position

4th House	Losses, humiliation, domestic unhappiness
5th House	Increase in prosperity and success, favours from superiors, birth of a child
6th House	Increase in expenditure, quarrels, anxiety
7th House	Monetary gains, happiness, birth of a child
8th House	Loss of money, misery, disputes
9th House	Success, birth of a child, prosperity and happiness
10th House	Losses, problems for children, illness
11th House	Promotion, prosperity, domestic happiness, birth of a child
12th House	Losses, grief, ill health

The transit results of Jupiter can also be predicted by another method. The transit of Jupiter in a trine *(Trikona)* house from the natal position (birth time position) of certain planets, and not from the natal Moon, is considered. When Jupiter transits the 5th or 9th house from the natal position of one of these planets in a nativity, the results are always auspicious.

1. When Jupiter transits the 5th or the 9th house from the natal Venus, positive effects will be felt by the native.
2. The native will secure good results in his educational pursuits if Jupiter traverses the 5th or 9th house from the natal Mercury.
3. The native will be blessed with wealth, happiness, and children if Jupiter transits the 5th or 9th house from his own natal position.
4. The native will receive favours from his superiors, an enhancement in income and reputation, and a promotion when Jupiter transits the 5th or 9th house from the natal position of Saturn.
5. When Jupiter transits the 5th or 9th house from the natal *Rahu*, the native will come out on top in litigation and controversies. He may perform auspicious ceremonies like a marriage during this period.

Venus:

1st House	Success, new position, enjoyment
2nd House	An increase in prosperity and happiness, birth of a child
3rd House	An increase in progress and happiness
4th House	Gains, birth of a child, happiness
5th House	Happiness, monetary gains, fame, birth of a child
6th House	Quarrels, losses, adversities
7th House	Trouble for wife, loss of money
8th House	Monetary gains, all-round prosperity, good health
9th House	An increase in prosperity and happiness
10th House	Quarrels, disgrace
11th House	Monetary gains and prosperity
12th House	Enjoyment, an increase in expenditure

Saturn:

1st House	Illness, loss of money, enmity, failures
2nd House	Loss of money, ill health, sorrow
3rd House	Money and position, success, happiness
4th House	Losses, misery, fear
5th House	Losses, mental worries, an increase in expenditure
6th House	All round prosperity and happiness
7th House	Ill health of wife and children
8th House	Troubles, losses, ill health
9th House	Troubles, enmity, ill health, unhappiness
10th House	Loss of honour and money, success in undertakings
11th house	Acquisition of money, honour and position
12th House	Quarrels, adversities, losses, ill health

Rahu* and *Ketu: During their transit from one house to another, *Rahu* produces results like that of Saturn, and *Ketu,* similar to that of Mars. However, unlike Saturn, *Rahu* is benefic in her transit through the 10th house.

21

Planets in Transit: The *Ashtakavarga* Chart

By virtue of their position in any horoscope planets are favourably or unfavourably disposed towards the twelve houses. Thus, a chart drawn to indicate the benefic and malefic influences of planets towards the houses is called the *Ashtakavarga* (A.V.) chart. A planet is said to be benefic in certain positions when counted from its own position, and from those of the other planets and *Lagna*. The *Ashtakavarga* system is found to be very useful when considered with the effect of planetary transits through the houses. *Rahu* and *Ketu* are exempted from consideration in this method.

Benefic Places of Planets in Their A.V. Charts

The places where a planet bestows benefits on the native may be conveniently marked by a crossmark. The number of crossmarks vary from as many as eight to as little as zero. The benefic places of each planet in its *Ashtakavarga* are discussed below:

The Sun: In the Sun's *Ashtakavarga*, the total number of benefic places are 48, and are as follows:

1, 2, 4, 7, 8, 9, 10, and 11, counted from his natal position
3, 6, 10, and 11 from the Moon
1, 2, 4, 7, 8, 9, 10, and 11 from Mars
3, 5, 6, 9, 10, 11, and 12 from Mercury

5, 6, 9, and 11 from Jupiter6, 7, and 12 from Venus
1, 2, 4, 7, 8, 9, 10, and 11 from Saturn
3, 4, 6, 10, 11, and 12 from the *Lagna*

The Moon: In the Moon's *Ashtakavarga*, the total number of benefic places are 49, and are as follows:

1, 3, 6, 7, 10, and 11 from her natal position
3, 6, 7, 8, 10, and 11 from the Sun
2, 3, 5, 6, 9, 10, and 11 from Mars
1, 3, 4, 5, 7, 8, 10, and 11 from Mercury
1, 4, 7, 8, 10, 11, and 12 from Jupiter
3, 4, 5, 7, 9, 10, and 11 from Venus
3, 5, 6, and 11 from Saturn
3, 6, 10, and 11 from the *Lagna*

Mars: The total number of benefic places of Mars in his *Ashtakavarga* are 39, and are as follows:

1, 2, 4, 7, 8, 10, and 11 from himself
3, 5, 6, 10, and 11 from the Sun
3, 6, and 11 from the Moon
3, 5, 6, and 11 from Mercury
6, 10, 11, and 12 from Jupiter
6, 8, 11, and 12 from Venus
1, 4, 7, 8, 9, 10, and 11 from Saturn
1, 3, 6, 10, and 11 from the *Lagna*

Mercury: In Mercury's *Ashtakavarga* the total number of benefic places are 54, and are as follows:

1, 3, 5, 6, 9, 10, 11, and 12 from its own position
5, 6, 9, 11, and 12 from the Sun
2, 4, 6, 8, 10, and 11 from the Moon
1, 2, 4, 7, 8, 9, 10, and 11 from Mars
6, 8, 11, and 12 from Jupiter
1, 2, 3, 4, 5, 8, 9, and 11 from Venus
1, 2, 4, 7, 8, 9, 10, and 11 from Saturn
1, 2, 4, 6, 8, 10, and 11 from *Lagna*

Jupiter: The total number of benefic places of Jupiter in his *Ashtakavarga* are 56, and are as follows:

1, 2, 3, 4, 7, 8, 10, and 11 from himself
1, 2, 3, 4, 7, 8, 9, 10, and 11 from the Sun
2, 5, 7, 9, and 11 from the Moon
1, 2, 4, 7, 8, 10, and 11 from Mars
1, 2, 4, 5, 6, 9, 10, and 11 from Mercury
2, 5, 6, 9, 10, and 11 from Venus
3, 5, 6, and 12 from Saturn
1, 2, 4, 5, 6, 7, 9, 10, and 11 from the *Lagna*

Venus: The total number of benefic places are 52 in Venus', *Ashtakavarga,* and are as follows:

1, 2, 3, 4, 5, 8, 9, 10, and 11 from herself
8, 11, and 12 from the Sun
1, 2, 3, 4, 5, 8, 9, 11, and 12 from the Moon
3, 5, 6, 9, 11, and 12 from Mars
3, 5, 6, 9, and 11 from Mercury
5, 8, 9, 10, and 11 from Jupiter
3, 4, 5, 8, 9, 10, and 11 from Saturn
1, 2, 3, 4, 5, 8, 9, and 11 from the *Lagna*

Saturn: In Saturn's *Ashtakavarga* the total number of benefic places are 39, and are as follows:

3, 5, 6, and 11 from the natal position of Saturn
1, 2, 4, 7, 8, 10, and 11 from the Sun
3, 6, and 11 from the Moon
3, 5, 6, 10, 11, and 12 from Mars
6, 8, 9, 10, 11, and 12 from Mercury
5, 6, 11, and 12 from Jupiter
6, 11, and 12 from Venus
1, 3, 4, 6, 10, and 11 from the *Lagna*

Example: Prepare the Ashtakavarga chart of the Sun for the horoscope given in Fig. 33.

To prepare the *Ashtakavarga* chart of the Sun for the above horoscope, draw an outline of the chart and fill the Sun's A.V. The Sun is auspicious in the 1st, 2nd, 4th, 7th, 8th, 9th, 10th, and 11th places from his position in the natal chart. In the Standard Nativity, the Sun is in Virgo. So Virgo is his natal or 1st position, Libra — 2nd, Sagittarius — 4th, Pisces — 7th, Aries — 8th, Taurus — 9th, Gemini — 10th, and Cancer — 11th. Place crossmarks in these signs.

The Sun is benefic in the 3rd, 6th, 10th, and 11th places from the Moon. The Moon is in Capricorn. Therefore, place crosses in Pisces, which is in the 3rd position from the natal Moon; Gemini in the 6th, Libra in the 10th, and Scorpio in the 11th.

The Sun is benefic in the 1st, 2nd, 4th, 7th, 8th, 9th, 10th, and 11th places from Mars. Mars is in Leo. Therefore, the benefic places for Mars are Leo in the 1st position, Virgo in the 2nd, Scorpio in the 4th, Aquarius in the 7th, Pisces in the 8th, Aries in the 9th, Taurus in the 10th, and Gemini in the 11th position.

The Sun's benefic places from Mercury are the 3rd, 5th, 6th, 9th, 10th, 11th, and 12th. Mercury is in Libra. Therefore, the benefic places are Sagittarius, Aquarius, Pisces, Gemini, Cancer, Leo, and Virgo, respectively.

The Sun is benefic in the 5th, 6th, 9th, and 11th places from Jupiter. Jupiter is in Leo. Therefore, the benefic places are Sagittarius, Capricorn, Aries, and Gemini, respectively.

The Sun is benefic in the 6th, 7th, and 12th places from Venus. Venus is in Libra. Therefore, the benefic places are Pisces, Aries, and Virgo, respectively.

6 xxxxxx	5 xxxxx	3 xxx	7 xxxxxxx
2 xx	THE SUN'S *ASHTAKAVARGA* CHART		3 xxx
3 xxx			2 xx
4 xxxx	4 xxxx	4 xxxx	5 xxxxx

Fig. 53

The Sun is benefic in the 1st, 2nd, 4th, 7th, 8th, 9th, 10th, and 11th places from Saturn. In the Standard Horoscope, Saturn is in Pisces. Therefore, the benefic places are Pisces, Aries, Gemini, Virgo, Libra, Scorpio, Sagittarius, and Capricorn, respectively.

Lastly, the Sun is benefic in the 3rd, 4th, 6th, 10th, 11th, and 12th places from the *Lagna*. The *Lagna* is Leo. Therefore, the benefic places for the Sun will be Libra, Scorpio, Capricorn, Taurus, Gemini, and Cancer, respectively. Placing crosses in all the aforesaid places, prepare the Sun's *Ashtakavarga* chart as shown overleaf. A.V. charts of all the planets can be prepared in the same manner.

Predictions Through *Ashtakavarga*

1. If a planet transits through any of the following places in an A.V. chart, benefic results will be produced:
   - a sign having a larger number of benefic crosses;
   - an *Upachaya* house (3rd, 6th, 10th, and 11th) counted from the *Lagna* or Moon;
   - its own house, a friendly, or exaltation sign.
2. If the crosses in any sign are less than 4, it is considered evil; more than 4 is considered good. As the number of crosses goes on increasing from 4 onwards, the benefic effects go on increasing proportionately; as the number goes on decreasing from 4, the harmful effects go on increasing. If the number is exactly 4, the transiting planet will have a neutral effect.
3. The A.V. chart of the Sun should be studied for prediction about the native's father, position, and influence; the Moon, for mother and mental happiness; Mars, for brothers, land, and property; Mercury, for business and profession; Jupiter, for education, finance, and children; Venus, for marriage, wife, and conveyances; and Saturn, for longevity, sorrow, and obstacles.

Based on the number of benefic crosses in the A.V. charts of each planet, the following general results may be noted:

The Sun. When the Sun transits through a house containing 8 benefic crosses in his *Ashtakavarga*, the native will enjoy prosperity. A house having 7 crosses predicts health and happiness; 6 crosses speak of fame; 5 crosses indicate monetary gains; 4 crosses signify both good and bad results; 3 and 2 crosses point to troubles; 1 cross symbolises diseases; and no crosses at all forebode calamity or death.

The Moon. Seven and eight crosses in a house denote various types of gains; 6 and 5 crosses show an association with noble and learned people, as well as mental happiness; 4 crosses indicate that the transiting planet has a neutral impact; 3 and 2 crosses mean monetary troubles and quarrels; 1 cross alludes to ill health; no crosses at all signify death or some other calamity.

Mars. Eight crosses in a house denote success, gain of wealth and property; 7 crosses predict happiness and prosperity; 6 crosses indicate that the native will seek favours from superiors; 5 crosses allude to fame; 4 crosses point to a neutral effect by the transiting planet; 3 crosses bespeak separation from brothers; 2 crosses demonstrate failure in undertakings; 1 cross indicates fear and illness; no crosses at all forebode death.

Mercury. Eight crosses in a house highlight an increase in position and prosperity; 7 crosses signify gain of wealth, knowledge, and happiness; 6 and 5 crosses show success in undertakings; 4 crosses have a neutral effect; 3 are indicative of mental worries; 2 and 1 both point to ill health; and the absence of crosses means losses and death.

Jupiter. Eight, seven, and six crosses are indicative of gain in position, money, and comforts; 5 crosses denote success in undertakings; 4 are neutral; 3 have a debilitating effect and lead to diseases; 2 crosses imply that the native will incur the displeasure of officials; 1 cross or no crosses at all are harmful and point to loss of wealth and death of relatives and children.

Venus. Eight and seven crosses show that the native will acquire luxuries and general prosperity; 6 and 5 crosses indicate marital or sexual bliss; 4 are neutral; 3 foretell misunderstandings and enmity; 2 and 1 crosses point to ill health, and loss of position; and no crosses at all will cause troubles for the native.

Saturn. Eight, seven, six, and five crosses show an increase in power and influence; 4 crosses are neutral; 3, 2, and 1 denote losses and ill health; no crosses at all are a negative sign, pointing to troubles or death.

Predictions Through *Sarvashtakavarga*

The *Sarvashtakavarga* (S.A.V.) chart denotes the consolidated number of benefic crosses in the A.V. charts of various planets. The S.A.V. chart is prepared by adding together the total number of benefic crosses in each house. The total number of crosses in all the houses of an S.A.V. chart should be 337.

1. A house can receive as many as 56 benefic crosses, and as little as zero. If the total number is between 25 and 30, the effects will be mixed or neutral. If the total number is above 30, the effects will be positive; and if less than 25, the effects will be harmful.
2. A larger number of benefic crosses in the ascendant promises sound health to the native. More crosses in the 2nd house indicate a good financial position; whereas, more in the 7th house signify matrimonial happiness. A greater number of crosses in the 9th house denote good fortune.
3. Add together the number of benefic crosses in the following houses counted from the *Lagna* in the S.A.V. chart:

   3rd, 7th, and 11th;
   4th, 8th, and 12th.

   If the total number of benefic crosses in the 1st group is more than in the 2nd, the native will be rich. If, on the other hand, the total number of crosses in the 2nd group is more than in the 1st, the native will have only modest means.
4. The native will enjoy happiness and prosperity if the total number of benefic crosses in the 11th house

exceeds that in the 10th; the total in the 12th is less than in the 11th; and the total in the *Lagna* is more than that in the 12th house.

5. Add together the benefic crosses in the following houses counted from the *Lagna*:
   1st, 4th, 7th, and 10th, representing early life;
   2nd, 5th, 8th, and 11th, representing middle life;
   3rd, 6th, 9th, and 12th, representing old age.

That part of the life of a native in which the total number of crosses is maximum denotes happiness and good fortune.

22

Some Important *Yogas* and Combinations

When planets are placed in particular positions or combinations they produce significant results for the native. These planetary combinations are called *Yogas*. There are hundreds of *Yogas*. Some of the important ones are enumerated below:

Adhi Yoga. This is caused if the benefic planets — Mercury, Jupiter, and Venus — are situated in the 6th, 7th, and 8th houses from the Moon. These planets should be present in any one, two, or in all the above-mentioned houses. A native with this *Yoga* will be very influential, healthy, and wealthy. He will possess no fear, disease, or enemy.

Amala Yoga. This *Yoga* is caused if the 10th house, either from the *Lagna* or the Moon, is occupied by a benefic planet. It makes a person moral, prosperous, and well-reputed.

Anapha Yoga. If any planet, other than the Sun, is placed in the 12th house from the Moon, this *Yoga* is caused. It makes the native generous, healthy, rich, and famous.

Apakeerti Yoga. If the 10th house is occupied by the Sun and Saturn, and aspected by malefics, the native will have a bad reputation.

Bhadra Yoga. This is caused by the disposition of Mercury in a quadrant in the sign Gemini or Virgo. A person born in this *Yoga* will be learned, wealthy and liberal; and will have a long life.

Budha-Aditya Yoga. If Mercury combines with the Sun, but not within 14°, this combination is caused. The native concerned will possess a keen intelligence and a good reputation.

Chandra-Mangala Yoga. If Mars is with the Moon, this *Yoga* is caused. It is a combination indicating a good financial position.

Chatussagara Yoga. This *Yoga* is caused when all the quadrants are occupied by planets. The person concerned will be well reputed and prosperous. He will enjoy health and comforts.

Daridra Yoga. The presence of the lord of the 11th house in the 6th, 8th, or 12th house gives rise to this *Yoga.* A person born in this combination will be poor and miserable, often in debt, and driven to committing mean deeds.

Duradhura Yoga. If there are planets, other than the Sun, on either side of the Moon, the native will be blessed with wealth and material comforts.

Dur Yoga. This *Yoga* is caused if the lord of the 10th house is placed in any one of the evil houses, that is, the 6th, 8th, or 12th house. The native will have to work hard, but, unfortunately, will not be able to derive the full benefit of his labour.

Gajakesari Yoga. The presence of Jupiter in a quadrant from the Moon causes this combination. A person with this combination will be intelligent, wealthy, famous, virtuous, and influential.

Hamsa Yoga. This combination is produced when Jupiter is posited in a quadrant in Cancer, Sagittarius, or Pisces. The native will have a well-formed body and a principled bent of mind. He will be learned and happy.

Kahala Yoga. The lords of the 4th and 9th houses should be in *Kendra* from each other, and the lord of the ascendant should be strong to give rise to this *Yoga.* The native will be daring and obstinate, and will hold an executive/administrative position.

Kapata Yoga. This combination is formed if the 4th house has a malefic planet and the lord of the 4th house is associated with, or aspected by, or surrounded with malefic planets. The person concerned will be evil minded and a hypocrite.

Kemadruma Yoga. This combination is formed when there are no planets on both sides of the Moon. The person will be poor, and possess a mean and obstinate disposition. His efforts will not bear much fruit.

Lakshmi Yoga. If the lord of the ascendant is strong and the lord of the 9th house occupies its own or exaltation sign in a *Kendra* or *Trikona*, the *Lakshmi Yoga* is formed. As a result, the native will have an attractive well-formed body, and will enjoy all the comforts of life.

Mahabhagya Yoga. In the case of a male, if the birth is during the day, and the Sun, the Moon, and the *Lagna* are in odd signs, the *Mahabhagya Yoga* is caused. In the case of a female, the birth should be at night and the Sun, the Moon, and the *Lagna* should be in even signs. A native born in this *Yoga* will be blessed with fortune, wealth, health, and children.

Malavya Yoga. Venus should occupy a quadrant in Taurus, Libra, or Pisces to form this *Yoga*. The native will have a strong mind, body, and character; and will be blessed with fame, fortune, wealth, a good wife, and children. He will enjoy worldly pleasures.

Ruchaka Yoga. Mars should occupy a quadrant in Aries, Scorpio, or Capricorn. The native will be a leader, possessing a robust body and generous disposition. He will acquire wealth and fame, and will be aggressive and arrogant.

Shakata Yoga. The Moon in the 6th, 8th, or 12th house from Jupiter gives rise to this *Yoga*. The person will be unlucky and miserable, and his life will be ordinary.

Shasha Yoga. This *Yoga* is caused if Saturn occupies a quadrant in Libra, Capricorn, or Aquarius. The native born in this *Yoga* will be rich but wicked in disposition.

Sunapha Yoga. If there is a planet, other than the Sun, in the 2nd house from the Moon, this *Yoga* will be caused. The native will be intelligent, famous, and prosperous.

Ubhayachari Yoga. This *Yoga* is caused if planets, other than the Moon, are present on both sides of the Sun. The concerned person will be wealthy, famous, and liked by all. He will be a good speaker and his body will be well formed.

Vasi Yoga. A benefic planet, other than the Moon, occupying the 12th house from the Sun, gives rise to *Shubhavasi Yoga.* The native will be happy-go-lucky and prosperous due to this *Yoga.* If a malefic planet occupies the 12th house *(Papavasi Yoga)*, the contrary results will be obtained.

Vasumati Yoga. This is caused when benefic planets occupy the *Upachaya* houses (3rd, 6th, 10th, 11th) counted from the *Lagna* or the Moon. The native will have plenty of wealth and property.

Veshi Yoga. If a planet, other than the Moon, occupies the 2nd house from the Sun, this *Yoga* is formed. If a benefic planet occupies the 2nd house from the Sun, the *Shubhaveshi Yoga* is formed. The person will be fortunate, happy, and rich. If, on the other hand, a malefic planet occupies the 2nd house from the Sun, *Papaveshi* is caused, which produces the opposite results.

23

Illustrative Horoscopes

Some miscellaneous horoscopes illustrating various personality traits or events in the life of their owners have been discussed in this chapter. Care has been taken to pinpoint astrological reasons for those attributes which have made these horoscopes distinctive.

A Managing Editor: The birth chart of a former managing editor employed in a publishing company can be seen in Fig. 54. The 3rd house in a horoscope is connected with writing, and editing. Note that the lord of the 3rd house, Mars, is in the ascendant with Neptune, indicating imaginative planning. Mercury, as lord of the 10th house (house of profession), is with the Sun, causing *Budha-Aditya*

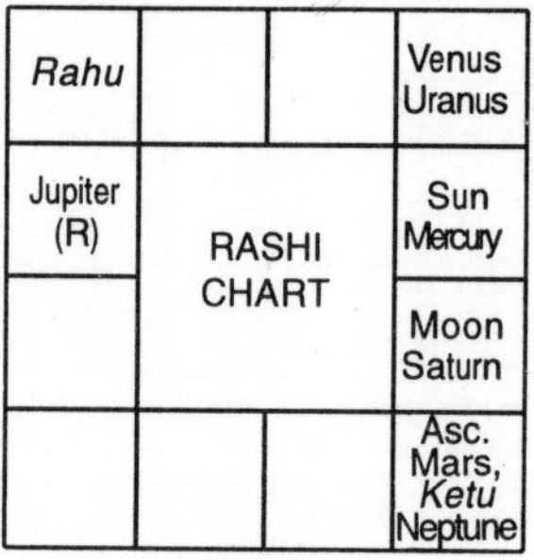

Fig. 54

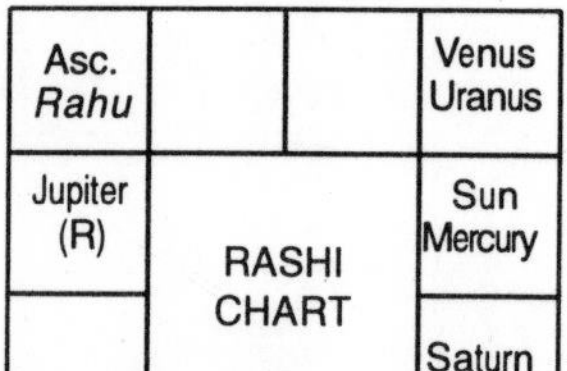

Fig. 55

Yoga. The sign Gemini in the 10th house shows professions involving intellectual skill and methodical planning. The 10th house is tenanted by Venus, and aspected by Jupiter.

An Administrative Officer: The birth chart of an additional district magistrate in the Provincial Civil Service can be seen in Fig. 55. The Moon, Mars, and Jupiter are auspicious planets for the native, with Pisces as ascendant. Note that both Mars and the Moon are aspecting the ascendant. Mars is also aspecting the house of profession. The Moon and Mars are further strengthened due to the birth of the native at night. Jupiter, as lord of the 1st and 10th houses, is retrograde, and, thus, strong. *Rahu's* aspect on the Sun has bestowed executive ability on the native.

A Case of Insanity: The horoscope of a mentally unsound person in Fig. 56 is an interesting one. The ascendant and the Moon (the significator of the mind and emotions) are afflicted by Saturn and Mars. The 5th house in a horoscope indicates intelligence. The lord of the 5th house, Mars, is in the company of *Rahu*, and aspected by Saturn. Both *Rahu* and Saturn represent an aberration of the mind. Saturn and the Moon are in *Kendra* to each other, thus further indicating an unsound state of the mind. The house of happiness (4th) is tenanted by the evil Saturn.

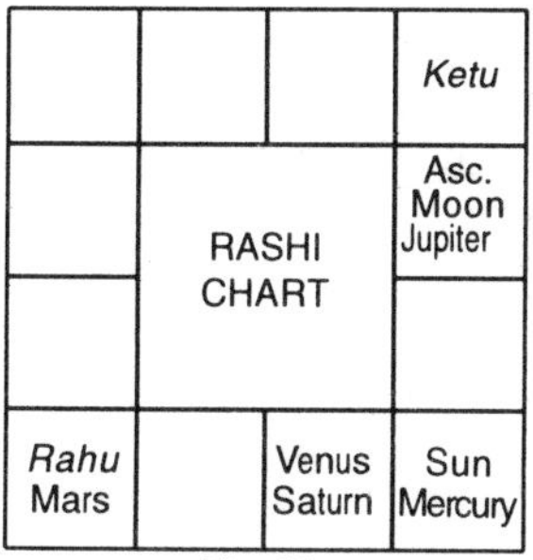

Fig. 56

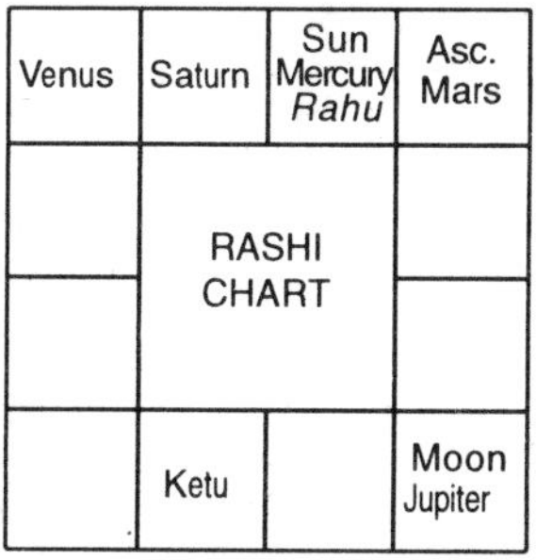

Fig. 57

Mahatma Gandhi's Assassin: The birth chart of Nathuram Vinayaka Godse, who committed the heinous crime of killing Mahatma Gandhi, the apostle of peace, can be seen in Fig. 57. Mark the presence of Mars in the ascendant, aspected by Saturn. Mars, as lord of the 6th and 11th houses, has become further cruel and violent. The Moon is also vitiated by *Rahu* and Mars. The Sun, as lord of the 3rd house and denoting courage, is strong, as its dispositor Venus is in exaltation. Mercury, the lord of the *Lagna* and Moon *Lagna,* has gone to the house of loss, in the company of two other malefics. The 12th house is surrounded by malefics. The death-inflicting planets for the Gemini ascendant are the Moon and Jupiter which are aspected by Mars and *Rahu.* No wonder that Godse himself was hanged to death after being found guilty of the crime.

Gen. K.M. Cariappa: The birth chart of the first Commander-in-Chief of free India, Gen. K.M. Cariappa, can be seen in Fig. 58. Note that the Sun, signifying courage, authority, and position, is in the ascendant, and is aspected by Saturn, lord of the ascendant. The Sun is strong as he receives motional strength by virtue of moving in the Northern course. Besides, he is lord of the Moon *Lagna* too. Mars, being retrograde, is very powerful. Mars, signifying the army, boldness, and valour, is aspecting the Sun as well as Jupiter (lord of the 3rd house, representing courage). The Sun, Jupiter, and Venus receive temporal strength. For natives of the Capricorn ascendant, Venus is *Yogakaraka* as she owns the 5th and 10th houses. Note the fine combination of Venus with the ascendant lord, Saturn, in a favourable house. Counted from the Moon, Venus is, again, the lord of the 10th house.

			Ketu
	RASHI CHART		Mars (R)
Asc. Sun			Moon
Rahu Mercury	Venus Saturn	Jupiter	

Fig. 58

Jupiter		Moon *Rahu*	Asc.
	RASHI CHART		
Sun Mercury	Mars, Venus Saturn *Ketu*		

Fig. 59

Zulfiqar Ali Bhutto — Former President of Pakistan: The birth chart of Zulfiqar Ali Bhutto, the former President of Pakistan, can be seen in Fig. 59. The death-inflicting planets for the Gemini ascendant are the Moon and Jupiter. Note that the Moon, as lord of the 2nd house, is in the house of loss along with *Rahu;* Jupiter, as lord of the 7th, is vitiated by the aspect of *Ketu.* Mars, Saturn and Venus, lords of the evil houses (6th, 8th, and 12th), are in mutual aspect with the malefic Moon. The intensely malefic Mars is aspecting the ascendant. Due to these evil combinations of planets, Bhutto suffered imprisonment and ignominy, followed by execution at the gallows.

Case of Suicide: The birth chart of a female who committed suicide by consuming poison, can be seen in Fig. 60. The death-inflicting planets for the Taurus ascendant are Mars and Jupiter, lords of the 7th and 8th houses, respectively. Note that Mars is aspecting Jupiter, the latter being in an inimical sign in the 2nd house. The 8th house from the Moon contains the malefic Mars. The ascendant is afflicted with *Rahu* and the lord of the ascendant, Venus, is aspected by an evil Jupiter.

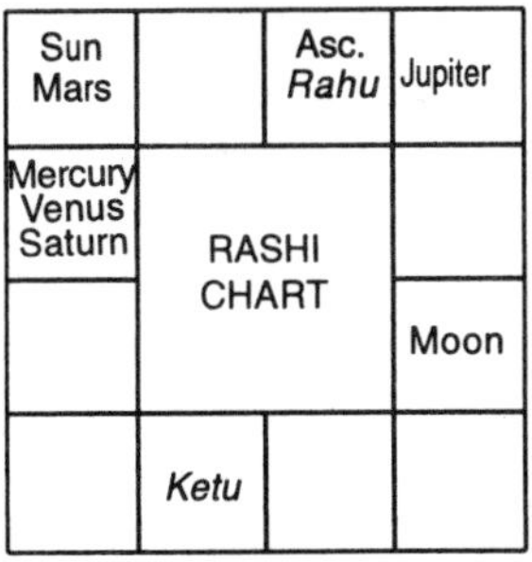

Fig. 60

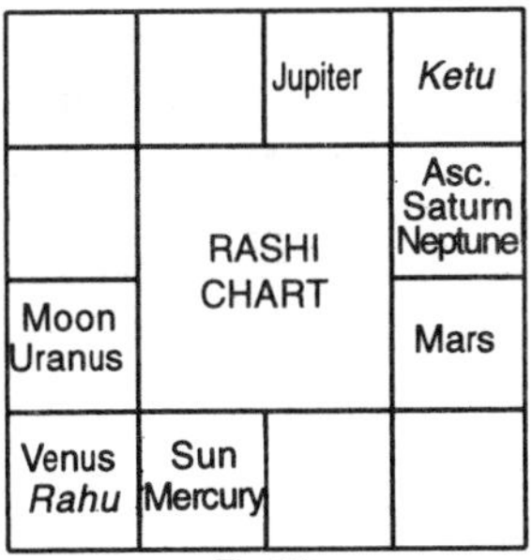

Fig.61

Indira Gandhi — Former Prime Minister of India: The birth chart of the former Prime Minister of India, Mrs Indira Gandhi, who was shot dead in a brutal and dastardly manner, can be seen in Fig. 61. The *Maraka* or death-inflicting planets for natives of the Cancer ascendant are the Sun and Saturn. Saturn, as lord of the 7th house, occupies the *Lagna*, surrounded by malefic planets. The *Lagna* lord Moon is in the 7th house. Mars is posited in the 2nd house from where it is aspecting the Sun, lord of the 2nd house. Reckoned from the Moon, Mars occupies the 8th house in aspect to malefic *Rahu.*

Rabindranath Tagore — Poet and Philosopher: The birth chart of the reputed poet and philosopher Rabindranath Tagore can be seen in Fig. 62. Note the auspicious and powerful exchange of places between the lords of the *Lagna* (Jupiter) and the 5th house (the Moon). The *Lagna* is strong, being aspected by the exalted Jupiter. The 5th house indicates intelligence, fame, and love for others. The Moon has no evil aspect; she signifies the mind, emotions, and imagination. There is a Sun-Mercury-Venus combination in the 2nd house, indicating the native's intellectual attainment in poetry, art, and music. Tagore was known and respected throughout the world as a philosopher, writer, and upholder of moral values.

V.P. Singh — Former Prime Minister of India: The horoscope of the Janata Dal leader and former Prime Minister V.P. Singh, can be seen in Fig. 63. Note that the exalted Jupiter, as lord of the 9th house, is placed in the ascendant, causing *Hamsa Yoga*. Thus, the *Lagna* is powerful though under the influence of *Rahu*. Remember that *Rahu* stands for diplomacy and politics. The *Lagna* lord, the Moon, is

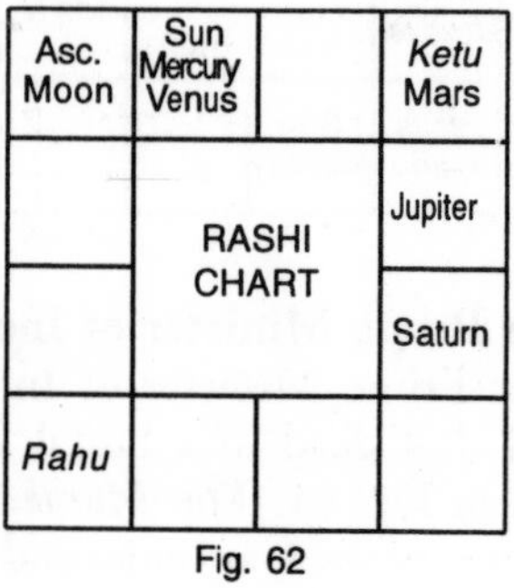

Fig. 62

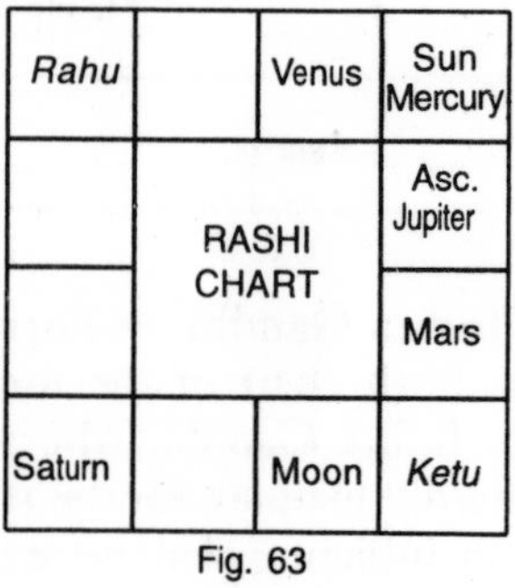

Fig. 63

aspecting the 10th house and the *Yogakaraka* Mars is aspecting the house of fortune. The Sun, representing political power, is in the house of loss, and is aspected by the intensely malefic Saturn.

Shri Ramakrishna Paramhamsa: The birth chart of Shri Ramakrishna Paramhamsa, one of the greatest saints of this country, is depicted in Fig. 64. He renounced everything to devote his life for the propagation of the Hindu religion and service of mankind. Note the fine combination for asceticism and high order of spirituality in his horoscope. The ascendant lord Saturn and the ascendant are powerfully aspected by Jupiter. Saturn is in the 9th house. The Sun and the Moon, representing the soul and the mind, respectively, are placed in the ascendant. Three planets — Venus, Mars, and Saturn — are in exaltation. Note also the presence of *Mahabhagya Yoga* as the Sun, the Moon, and the ascendant are in an odd sign, while the birth took place during the day.

Kapil Dev — the Famous Cricketer: The birth chart of the famous cricketer of international fame, Kapil Dev, can be seen in Fig. 65. The ascendant Aries is indicative of his bold and active temperament. The ascendant lord Mars is in the ascendant, causing *Ruchaka Yoga*. Mars signifies stamina, enthusiasm, sports. Note the presence of the lords of the 5th, 10th, and 11th houses in the house of fortune, indicating fame, honour, and gains, respectively. The lord of the house of fortune, Jupiter, is aspecting the house of wealth, while the ascendant lord Mars is aspecting the benefic Jupiter.

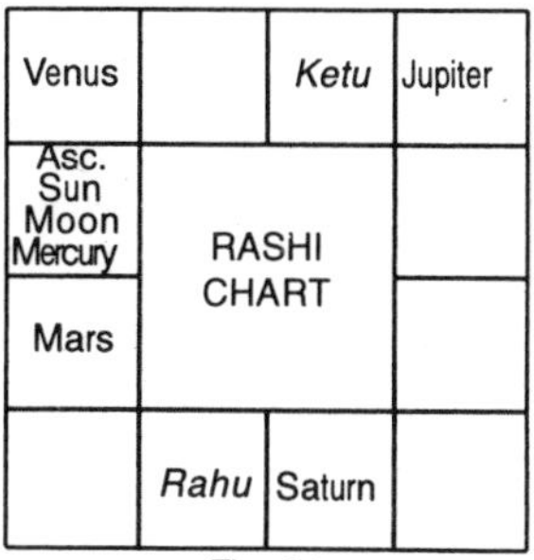

Fig. 64

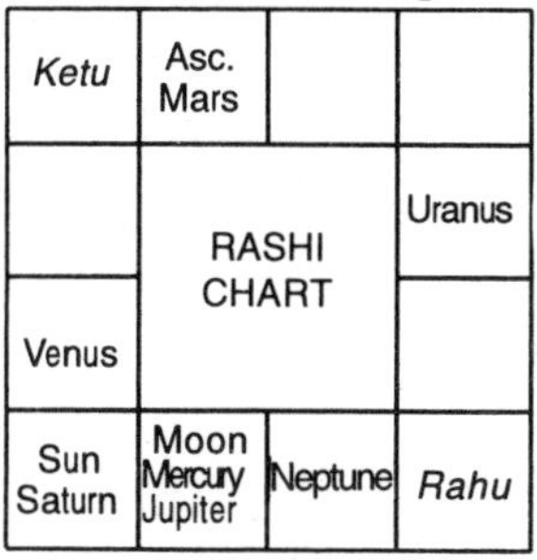

Fig. 65

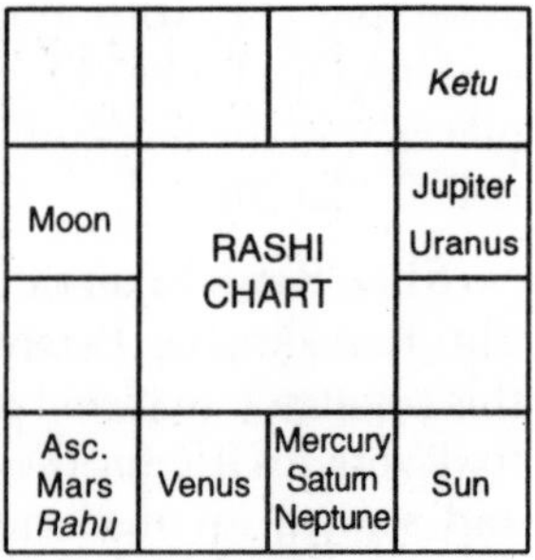

Fig. 66

Rekha — the Well-Known Movie Star: The birth chart of the famous film star, Rekha, is seen in Fig. 66. Venus, signifying acting, dancing, and feminine grace, is powerfully aspected by an exalted Jupiter. Mars, as lord of the 5th house, indicating name and fame, is in the ascendant, and is aspecting the lord of the ascendant, Jupiter. The Sun, as the lord of the 9th house, receives temporal and directional strength. An exalted Saturn (lord of the 2nd house, indicating wealth) and Mercury (lord of the 10th house, indicating profession) are together in a favourable house, showing a successful career and an abundant income. The Moon is in a favourable house from the ascendant, while Jupiter and Venus are in favourable houses from the Moon.

An Astrologer: The birth chart of a well-known astrologer and author of several books on astrology, is seen in Fig. 67. The ascendant is powerful as it is occupied by its lord, Jupiter. Jupiter is retrograde and is lord of the 10th house. The Moon, as lord of the 5th house, and representing name and fame, is under the benefic influence of Jupiter. Mars, the lord of the 2nd and 9th houses, is exalted in a favourable house. The 3rd house indicates writing. Note that the lords of the 3rd house from the ascendant and the Moon are Venus and Saturn, respectively, and are in aspect to each other. Besides, there is an exchange of places between the lords of the 2nd and 11th houses, indicating significant wealth and gains.

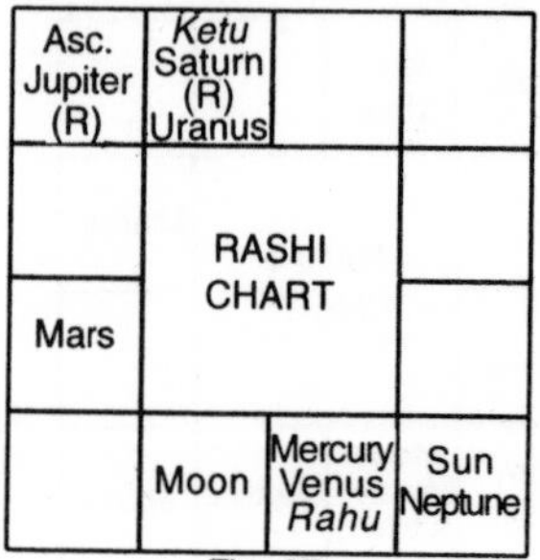

Fig. 67

A Case of Paralysis: The birth chart of a boy crippled below the knees with polio, is seen in Fig. 68. Note that the lord of the ascendant is debilitated and sandwiched between the malefic planets. There are evil aspects of Mars and Saturn on the ascendant. Mars, representing the limbs, is in the house of disease. Saturn, the significator of paralysis, is aspecting Mars. The 11th and 12th houses represent the legs, ankles, and feet. Note that Mercury, lord of the 11th house, is with Saturn, under the evil influence of *Rahu*. The Moon, as lord of the 12th house, is surrounded by malefics.

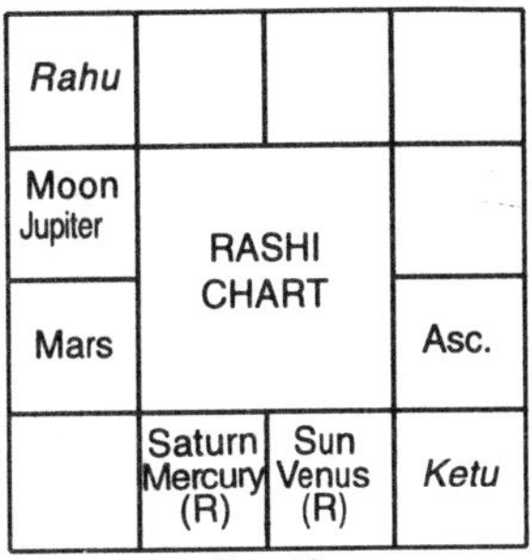

Fig. 68

Glossary

Amavasya. The day of the New Moon, the 15th *tithi* in the dark half.

Ashtakavarga. A chart indicating the number of benefic effects of planets in various houses.

Asta. Combustion. Planets in intimate conjunction with the Sun are subject to combustion and become powerless.

Ayanamsha. This is the distance the first point of Aries and the Vernal Equinox.

Bhava. Each of the 12 houses of the zodiac.

Bhava Sandhi. Junction point of the two adjoining houses.

Dakshinayana. A period of six months when the Sun moves from the sign Cancer to the sign Sagittarius.

Dasha. Dashas are the periods during which good or bad effects of the planets are felt by an individual.

Ecliptic. The path along which the Sun moves.

Gochara. Movement of planets through various houses of the zodiac counted from the moon at the time of birth.

Janma Nakshatra. The *Nakshatra* in which the moon is placed at the time of birth.

Krishna Paksha. The dark fortnight of the lunar month — the day after the full Moon to the day of the new Moon.

Lagna. The sign that rises in the East at the time of birth.

Mangalika. This refers to a person in whose birth chart Mars is placed in the 1st or 2nd, 4th, 7th, 8th, or 12th house from the Lagna, the Moon or Venus.

***Moolatrikona* Signs.** Strong positions of the planet, similar to those of exaltation.

Nakshatras. The ecliptic (the path of the Sun) has 27 equal parts which are called *Nakshatras.*

Navamsha. A *Navamsha* is 1/9th of a zodiac sign.

***Neecha* Signs.** Debilitated signs.

***Nirayana* System.** The system, as employed by Indian Astrology, which considers the zodiac to be fixed.

Pada. A quarter of a *Nakshatra.*

Poornima. This refers to the day of the full Moon, the 15th *tithi* in the bright half.

Rahu* and *Ketu. The ascending and descending Nodes of the Moon, that is, the points at which the path of the Moon in the celestial sphere cuts that of the Sun.

Rashi. A zodiacal sign.

Samvat. A Lunar year consisting of 12 lunar months.

Sarvashtaka Varga. This deals with the benefic crosses that appear in the A.V. charts of various planets.

***Sayana* System.** The Western system of astronomy that recognizes the zodiac as movable.

Shukla Paksha. Each lunar month consists of two *Pakshas. Shukla Paksha* is the bright fortnight, — the day of the new Moon to the day of the full Moon.

Significator (*Karaka*). When each planet signifies or promotes certain traits and matters associated with an individual, it is called a significator *(Karaka).*

Tithi. A Lunar day.

***Uchcha* Signs.** Exalted signs.

Uttarayana. A period of six months when the Sun moves from the zodiacal sign Capricorn to the sign Gemini.

Vargottamamsha. The position of a planet when it occupies the same sign both in the *Rashi* and *Navamsha* charts.

Vedha. Places where obstacles fall across the path of planets.

***Vimshottari Dasha* system.** A period of 120 years, with each planet being assigned a fixed number of years.

Yoga. Planetary combinations.

Also In Orient Paperbacks

The Book of the Zodiac
Cheiro's You and Your Star

In this book, "I have set out, not only the basic meaning of each month as handed down to mankind by the observations of astrologers from far distant ages to the present day, but also the meaning ascribed to each day of the year from the influence of the planets according to Chaldean Numerology."

'As far as I know, this is the first time that these combinations have ever been given to the world in an attempt to make what may be called Zodiacal Astrology of assistance to the vast mass of humanity who have not the time or the inclination to go into mathematical calculations that would be necessary in working out any other astrological system.'

— *Cheiro*
From the Foreword of the book.

Complete and unabridged authorised edition of Count Louis Hamon's, better known as 'Cheiro', classic work on astrology.

Also in Orient Paperbacks

Kabala
Ancient Secrets of Numerology

Sepharial

Kabala is an ancient work of Jewish mysticism and occult lore. Unlike other ancient systems of numerology which limit their study to the influence of numbers 0-to-9, the Jewish or the Hebrew Kabala extends the significance and interpretation of numbers to twenty-two, linking these with the twenty-two letters of the Hebrew alphabet.

In this book Sepharial explains how the knowledge of numbers, their sympathies and antipathies, discord and harmonies, can be applied in a variety of ways in our daily affairs with rewarding and profitable results.

"...explains how one can profit on speculative activities and turn the financial wheel of fortune in his favour by finding out his lucky and money numbers based on the day of the week and the hour in which one is born."

The Hindu

Orient Paperbacks
5A/8, Ansari Road, New Delhi-110 002
www.orientpaperbacks.com